INSIGHTS OF AN
AMERICAN INVESTMENT MANAGER
—— IN ——
HONG KONG

BROOK McCONNELL

Copyright © 2020 by Brook McConnell.

All rights reserved. No part of this publication may be reproduced, distributed or transmitted in any form or by any means, including photocopying, recording, or other electronic or mechanical methods, without the prior written permission of the publisher, except in the case of brief quotations embodied in critical reviews and certain other noncommercial uses permitted by copyright law.

The contents of this book do not constitute an investment recommendation. As such, this book does not contain all information that a prospective investor may desire in evaluating an investment strategy or individual investment. Each investor must rely on his or her own examination of an investment strategy or individual investment, including the merits and risks involved in making an investment decision. Prior to making an investment decision, a prospective investor should consult his or her own counsel, accountants, and other advisors to evaluate the merits of an investment strategy or individual investment. Additionally, any discussion of the past performance of any investment strategy or individual investment should not be relied on as a guarantee of future performance, and no warranty of future performance is intended or implied.

Cover Design by 100Covers.com
Interior Design by FormattedBooks.com

DEDICATION

To my late father, Dick McConnell

ACKNOWLEDGEMENTS

Much effort was contributed by my editor, Thomas Farrell, who worked with me for months on the manuscript editing. Special thanks to two friends, Hugh Peyman and Steve Lazar, who both rendered their writing and editing skills for not only reviewing but giving me invaluable insights into the final edition. This book is also dedicated to my son (Brook), daughter (Molly), my two 'Hong Kong daughters' (Desiree and Denise) and especially my beloved wife, Karolyn, which, without her patience and love, I couldn't have finished this book.

PREFACE

I have attempted to present an analysis in this book based on my own experiences as an American living in Hong Kong, visiting Chinese companies, and attending conferences throughout China for nearly three decades. During those studious years of learning, I've written monthly about my findings. It is from a firsthand perspective that I've observed the rise of China's living standards and the stature it has gained as a world power today. There were plenty of doubters along the way and many who quickly moved to grab low hanging opportunities presented in China as it laboriously restructured, yet significantly transformed, its economy.

Just as I finished the final editing of this manuscript, the world turned upside down overnight by the coronavirus pandemic. Though the immensity of the virus impact has swept away all the front-page issues I discuss and disseminate throughout this book, I would wager these same issues and new ones will emerge once the pandemic stabilizes.

Ray Dalio, founder of the world's largest hedge fund (Bridgewater), recently turned to history to summarize his outlook about China. He presents a sequential outline of the world's evolution beginning with the Dutch empire, continuing through the rise and decline of the British empire, and into the US empire. From there he presents the US empire's rise and early decline into the rise of the present Chinese empire. He concludes in *The Changing World Order*:

> "For the first time in my lifetime, the United States is encountering a rival power. China has become a competitive power to the United States in a number of ways and is growing at a faster rate than the US. If trends continue, it will be stronger than the United States in most of the most important ways that an empire becomes dominant. (Or at the very least, it will become a worthy competitor.) I have seen both countries up close for most of my life, and I now see how conflict is increasing fast, especially in the areas of trade, technology, geopolitics, capital, and economic/political/social ideologies. I can't help but wonder how these conflicts, and the changes in the world order that will result from them, will transpire in the years ahead and what effects that will have on us all..."[1]

The storyline of the Chinese economy remains the same. Long term trends in technology, consumption, and market consolidation may be disrupted by trade wars and viruses, but they won't disappear. China will endure and be particularly pertinent to equity investors over the next decades.

This book is about those developments.

---

1 Ray Dalio, "The Changing World Order," *The Changing World Order* (blog), LinkedIn, March 25, 2020, https://www.linkedin.com/pulse/changing-world-order-ray-dalio-1f/.

INTRODUCTION

On a warm September morning, we drove through the guarded gates of the factory compound and made our way up to the lobby entrance. It was 1992, and this was our first visit into mainland China. Having departed early that morning from the central business district on Hong Kong Island, we were now two hours across the border.

The place was immaculate. Elderly women, with large-brimmed straw hats orbiting their heads, swept the grounds spotless—brooms of bamboo swinging like clock-time to remove any traces of dust. This was the production base for a major manufacturer of floppy disks, and in the early nineties the three-and-a-half-inch plastic square was one of the hottest selling commodities. Back then, every personal computer had an injection port to read these diskettes.

Our hosts led us through the lobby doors and deep into the recesses of the building. Hallway after hallway, pristine and ordered, like some highly-efficient palace. My father and I shared a growing sense of curiosity, as if we were the first Americans ever to enter these corridors. We were on the way to meet with management of the listed

Hong Kong company. The first of what would become hundreds of these visits all over the country.

My anticipation was running high. All along the journey that morning, my preconceived visions about what we were headed into dominated my thoughts: a place where the working conditions were full of despair and agony, summoned from the pages of a Steinbeck novel. I readied myself for the inevitable queasiness that would come when we witnessed the scenes of immense toil, misery, and suffering I expected to find inside these factories—the notorious sweat shops I had been reading about years before we even left for Hong Kong.

Finally, we came to a large room upstairs where we met with company managers who smoked Chinese cigarettes and drank tea as they discussed the manufacturing operations. The general manager was a Hong Kong resident who spent his workweek running the factory in Guangdong Province and his weekends back in Hong Kong with family. He spoke clear English, probably from having dealt with Westerners like ourselves, from the days the factory was located in Hong Kong. I tracked what he was saying carefully, but kept wondering what the working conditions would be like once we toured the rest of the compound. An uneasiness was building in my gut.

After the meeting, we moved downstairs and outside to the adjoining factory. As we entered the great hall, that leery and apprehensive feeling shot through me. I swallowed in anticipation of what we were about to see. But upon entering the first assembly floor, I was immediately struck at how it spread out impressively before us. It was huge—about half the size of a contemporary Walmart. Three long assembly lines of young Chinese girls flowed down the open warehouse, all seated at station workbenches and dressed in blue smocks with surgical-knit hair pieces. An assembly belt ran between each of the stations with partially assembled floppy disk pieces being conveyed further and further along.

The factory floor hummed with activity. As we walked down the aisles between the assembly lines, I watched the diligence and skilled maneuvers of the young women working—assembling the springs inside each of the disk cases and then placing the discs back on the assembly belt for the next procedure. Most of them were bent over, deep in their work, like pianists lost in their compositions. Occasionally, they might glance up as we passed, their slightly suspicious, curious eyes tracking us. I watched them watch us and then glance back at each other, acknowledging some hidden message in the space between.

But something was off. Something I simply hadn't expected. These workers didn't seem unhappy! Wasn't this one of the epicenters of the most repressive and authoritarian regimes in the world? Why weren't their faces painted or smudged in soot and sweat? Why weren't their clothes old and tattered? And where were the slave drivers? Men, belted with knives and chains, standing above all the workers, screaming in nasal Mandarin? Maybe the whole thing was kept hidden behind a vast curtain, concealed momentarily for our expected arrival and inspection. Whatever it was, the destitution I expected wasn't the case at all. The storyline had changed and my schema was transforming right in front of me.

Outside, in the hallway, the manager from Hong Kong confided in us a few revealing aspects of life there at the factory. Yes, indeed, these three hundred girls inside the first assembly line were happy employees (there were eight assembly lines within the walled factory compound). Foreign factories in China paid wages at twenty-two cents an hour, plus room and board, which was high above domestic factory compensations. Most employees worked eight to ten hours a day, seven days a week, with overtime. Within two years' time, the manager explained, each of these young women could accumulate enough savings to return to their home province and buy a place for themselves. No mortgage. Cash payment only.

News of their affluence, after returning to their families in the hinterlands, would spread like wildfire over a dry plain. Unheard of fortunes were being earned working in southern China factories. Paramount Leader Deng Xiaoping's opening to foreign investment in the Special Economic Zone (SEZ) of Guangdong Province was attracting rural youth like a magnet. This was the start of China's great opening and it was mainly funded with direct investment from established Hong Kong Chinese manufacturers. Hong Kong factory owners were rapidly relocating their entire Western export-oriented operations back to their 'home' towns across the border. The great worker migration had just begun. Countless masses of young men and women from all parts of China's countryside headed to the new economic zones in the south for the long-absent opportunity of 'fantastic' wages and 'exorbitant' riches.

The wealth, he said, was on display. Out in the courtyard parking lot stood a tangle of one-speed bicycles, thousands of them stacked up on top of each another. As soon as enough savings were accrued, workers splurged to buy 'luxury' items. Bicycles were status symbols signifying freedom, joy, and leisure. But one of the biggest thrills for the young women was to gather under a light bulb at night for socializing. In their hometowns, he explained, they had no electricity. Evenings were cloaked in darkness. Chinese teenagers didn't go to malls to carouse at night—there simply weren't any malls. Nothing stayed open after sunset. Roads went unpaved, and no taxis or buses ran. There were no fast food restaurant chains except for a few plastic chairs and tables positioned on the sidewalk outside a family home.

There were no bars, no entertainment venues, no movies shown except the occasional state-sponsored film projected onto a white-cloth screen in some small open-air room.

At the factories, however, when shifts ended, the atmosphere turned ecstatic. The girls relaxed, came together to commiserate, tell jokes, and talk about their lives. They were fed well, by their standards, and given comfortable bunk beds in dormitories (room and board was a legal requirement for foreign factories operating in China). Hanging above them in the late hours like a promise in the night, as the young women enlightened each other about the many paths of life, was always a bright-white glow from an iridescent light bulb.

The assembly line workers were mostly dark-haired women in their early twenties. Not only were the women more manageable, the manager explained, but they had the manual dexterity, with smaller hands and fingers, to best undertake the exacting work quickly. Young men were assigned heavier tasks, either employed at loud stamping machines or in the packaging and transportation sections.

Though the dorms for the young women and men were in separate buildings, I knew there had to be commingling. This, I found out, the company spent a great deal of effort and time trying to manage. On walks outside around the buildings, we'd see couples holding hands, but the managers had strict rules keeping workers separate. They wanted to avert any incidents, dramas, or episodes that might bring in the town officials, scrutinizing and disrupting the 24/7 operations.

Later that hazy afternoon, as we started back through the countryside and villages, I felt as though I was wandering along the edges of some dream-like and surreal world. The landscape was one vast industrial construction site, mile after mile of new factories sprawled out before us. These newly built plants churned out millions of manufactured goods for export. The products were sold at extremely competitive prices on world markets from the considerable advantage of cheap labor and land costs offered on the mainland.

Masses of people crowded the countryside. Residents seemed to be everywhere along the roads, pressed close together, shoulder to shoulder. Our driver navigated through the crisscrossing patterns we encountered without slowing down. I sat in the back gripping the arm-rest and looked out the side window, not able to bring myself to watch all the near-misses happening up in front.

On the drive we passed long rows of low-rise, cookie-cutter homes, all fronting east. Peasant farmers crossed over the fresh four-lane roads we were traveling, rakes slung over their shoulders, seemingly oblivious to all oncoming traffic. Occasionally older men mixed among the throngs of people, dressed in drab grey buttoned-up Mao suits, and older women appeared in even drabber pajamas. They'd be standing along the roadside, idly watching the hectic traffic. But many, mostly younger Chinese pedestrians on those one-gear bicycles, were dressed in the latest fashions paid for by factory work earnings. After studying their faces, I decided they must have been heading home, with their plastic orange bags tied onto their bike racks, filled with fresh dinner preparations from the local market. I guessed the insides of their homes were basic with only the simplest of appliances. Air conditioning was just beginning to reach the masses in the hot humid southern Province. Though China's farmers were poor by any Western measure, they were not destitute. Life was tough for the majority of citizens, but a month's worth of rice cost just two yuan (less than thirty cents) which assured sustenance. Their existence was harsh, but it was not intolerable.

The grinding and impoverished living conditions in China would be quite difficult, if not totally incomprehensible, for non-Chinese foreigners to digest. As a rule, a Westerner's first visit into the country was typically a wrenching shock, akin to arriving at the spaceport town of Mos Eisley on the planet Tatooine, where the famous Star Wars' bar-room scene took place. Nevertheless, conditions and life were improving at an astoundingly rapid pace in the large coastal urban areas, particularly in the newly created special economic zones in southern China.

The young women who worked in the factories, dressed in smart uniforms, were the precursors to China's rejuvenation and renaissance. The resurrection of a lost generation, encumbered by the unfortunate 'iron rice bowl' experiment under Mao, was visible everywhere. China was in the early stages of becoming a major, global manufacturing powerhouse.

• • •

My first trip into the Peoples Republic of China was an eye-opener. The floppy disk factory was our initial foray into seeking investment values outside the US. China factories were making profits and the low labor wages were actually quite generous for mainland Chinese workers. Share prices of the listed Hong Kong companies—those just beginning to move their operations into China—were also cheap by almost every standard of valuation. Advancing profits looked assured with the improved cost structures of cheap land and labor.

My father and I both concluded we wanted to be a part of this historic evolution. We began laying plans to invest in this yet-discovered growth opportunity by launching an investment firm in the financial district of Hong Kong. It was like a light bulb coming on above our heads.

Dad had been a well-known, successful investment professional on Wall Street. My previous career was an eight-year stint as a stockbroker with PaineWebber and five years with a Wall Street money management firm in New York City. He was sixty-seven and I was forty when we considered moving to Asia. The old man was a tough customer, a smart money man, and all along had been my mentor and best friend.

What Dad astutely observed that day was that the Western-trained, Hong Kong manufacturers were the most logical beneficiaries of what China was offering: abundant low-cost land and anxious-to-work workers, all with implicit government backing. As they would know best, founders and managers based in Hong Kong were undoubtedly the ones to follow as they spoke the language of the land in all its connotations. Over the ensuing years, we visited hundreds more of these listed companies in order to develop confidence and deeper understanding of this new empire.

・・・

I wrote this book with the intent of recording our company's origins, as well as providing insight into our investment strategies for those interested in investing with us. During the writing process, it became apparent that my impressions and observations about living in the modern enclave of Hong Kong were a natural outgrowth of such an intent. These last twenty-seven years have been an on-the-job history course for one of the most dramatic rebirths and increases in living standards ever recorded in mankind's history. My firsthand impressions and observations stem from actual events and people I encountered throughout my fortunate time living in the Far East. They may not be wholly accurate, nor flattering, as they're drawn from the memory of an outsider during the nearly three decades I spent there. But if nothing else, they are honest commentaries of the many encounters and insights I gained living in a foreign land, and I've tried to be impartial to both sides of the philosophical and economic spectrum that covers the East and West. The future for China is compelling; I will describe just how compelling an investment it is through the course of this book.

I am indebted to my late father for his enthusiasm, guidance, support and wisdom. He imparted much to my learning while we built a life and business together far from our native homeland.

We were exhilarated and enthusiastic with what we were beholding, and that perspective hasn't changed. The Special Administrative Region (SAR) of Hong Kong, with its contemporary conveniences and advanced infrastructure, was ostensibly the most advantageous center to start building our new venture.

CHAPTER 1

FROM THE BEGINNING

I was born outside Charlottesville, Virginia, in August 1952 in a small town called Ivy, located in Albemarle County. Most people living in the bucolic countryside of Albemarle are steeped in the tradition and lore of Thomas Jefferson's homeland, but I always had a wanderlust for the frontiers, like Meriwether Lewis of the Lewis and Clark expedition. Lewis was also born in Ivy on an August day long ago. In 1803, when President Thomas Jefferson concluded a deal with France to buy the "Louisiana Purchase," he tasked Lewis with exploring the vast and unknown frontiers of northwest America to find out what he had bought. This is a venture to which I can easily relate.

My parents moved from Virginia to Connecticut in the early 1960s while I was in elementary school. Though Dad was commuting to Wall Street for work, his upbringing in the countryside drew him to acquire a thousand acres in western Vermont—a five-hour drive north from our Connecticut home. I spent many seasons at our farm in Vermont, learning to shoot, hunt, fish, and ride motorcycles. Back then, Vermont was unpolluted and still very remote. The locals were authentic people and weren't desensitized by television or the internet. Our rural neighbors became close family friends; their genuine and unstressed nature stood out in stark contrast to the many city dwellers beginning to immigrate to the Green Mountains.

Our property annexed a lone dairy farm and we allowed the farmer there to graze his cattle on our fields. My brothers and I often walked to the barn at milking times to help. We were outdoors all summer long. The Honda company had just invaded the US with a $199, 55 cc motorcycle, which was a hot-selling item. Dad couldn't resist buying one and we rode that motorcycle over rough fields and up mountainsides. On hot summer afternoons we'd cool-off by hand-fishing for trout in the streams below our house. We'd camp in two-man tents in the forests, gig frogs at night in the nearby lake, shoot our high-powered rifles at sticks of dynamite strapped to floats in the pond, and when summer turned to fall and fall to winter we'd ski the snow-covered hills and mountains. I loved the adventure of hunting for deer, ruffled grouse, bear, and shooting varmint woodchucks. As teenagers, my brothers and I spent weekends 'stalking' female companionship in the nearby towns of Pawlet and Wells, Vermont; and Granville, New York. It was a healthy life.

My desire to be in the mountains led to my attending a boarding school on the other side of the state called Vermont Academy. VA was intensively academic and athletically focused. I excelled there under the strict disciplines, and credit much of my successes in later life to that three-year stint in Saxtons River. While there, I played drums in the basement of the school dining hall with a band that gigged at the dances. Our lead guitarist, Joe, who left school before I did, asked if I might join him in the new band he was organizing, but dad said there would be no more drums in my future. At the end of the year I would go off to college and Joe would start the band called Aerosmith. Perhaps the first of many roads diverged in a wood.

After graduation, three classmates and I took a seventeen-day canoe trip on the Mississippi River starting from its source located in upper Minnesota, down to Dubuque, Iowa. A 450-mile trip, sleeping on the muddy banks in tents. The first nights on the river were nightmares as clouds of mosquitoes forced us back into our canoes and out into the middle of the water. It rained a lot on our journey, soaking us and all our gear. The wind, strong enough to push our canoes upstream against the currents, constantly blew in our face, even when we rounded bends in the river. It was a struggle not to give up against all the elements, and I finished the trip no longer a boy.

My college years were just as educational and exciting. I decided on Denver University because of its proximity to the Rocky Mountains, where I could ski and explore. DU was known as a party school but recognized for its top-rated business program and renowned graduate law school. Had I not had the discipline instilled in me from Vermont Academy, I doubt I would have lasted long at DU. During the summer I worked various jobs, including laboring at a lumber yard in Manchester, Vermont, and organizing a company with my fraternity brothers to paint houses in the shadows of the Denver skyline.

One summer break, I worked on a major oil company's onshore/offshore drilling section based in Paris, France. I assisted the president of Schlumberger's Forex/Neptune division with their English translation communiques. During the summer, the company sent me to Stavanger, Norway, to board a helicopter for a two-week stint on their North Sea oil rig. The huge pentagon-shaped iron mass actually floated on the ocean, with five long anchor chains attached to the sides. The decks and living quarters were a hundred feet above the ocean's surface. At all times, the drill pipe would bash back and forth against the steel floor as if it were moving but it was actually the movement of the entire rig floating on the sea. If you fell overboard you'd have twenty minutes in the freezing surf before hyperthermia set in and death.

I helped a Brit with the more mundane chores of cleaning rooms each morning, and at night we'd play ping pong. He told me something interesting which I never forgot. Wildcatting for oil was a high risk/high reward venture and the captain was the only one on board who knew whether the drilling hit pay dirt or not. As soon as he got the results, he'd make a coded phone call to the chairman of the company onshore. If oil was discovered, he told the chairman it was a nice day, even if the weather was miserable. If the drilling came up dry, he'd say it was cloudy out there. Then the captain would hang up and make a second call to his broker.

I asked the captain about life out on the open seas and he relayed stories of storms with fifty-foot waves bashing loudly into the hull of the rig during winter storms. His biggest concern, though, was hitting a gas reservoir while drilling, leaking the gas bubbles from the ocean floor up to the rig. Bubbles would cause the surface water tension to break down and the whole rig would sink immediately. When I asked what he'd do if such an event occurred, he told me he'd cut three anchor lines and start towing the rig with the two anchors as fast as possible.

I decided after that trip I'd rather get my ulcers behind a desk than out on the wild ocean of the North Sea.

• • •

As an English literature major, I was the only liberal arts student in our fraternity. One of our classmates was Condoleezza Rice, who became Secretary of State during George W. Bush's tenure, and whose father was a dean. Our fraternity, Tau Kappa Epsilon, was once embroiled in a fireworks war with the neighboring frat houses, whereby Condoleezza's father, Dean Rice, called in our president to reprimand us and have us expelled. Luckily, our president was smart and agile enough to get us off, saying our actions would never lead to any more disturbances on campus.

Naturally, we never stopped our collegiate escapades, and even initiated a new fad that was gaining traction in the US at the time—running naked through public places. Local TV broadcasters were astonished and dumbstruck by our antics; evening news stations captured brief scenes of streakers running free around campus. At one point, during mid-period of an intense DU hockey game, our fraternity struck the ice (donning masks in case Dean Rice was in the audience) to the roars of five thousand fans attending that evening. For a short time we held the record for streaking in front of the most onlookers, but that was soon broken by a group of naked parachutists who jumped above the University of Illinois and landed amidst a huge horde of spectators on the quad. But as the saying goes: "Once we were kings…"

After college, the need to find a job could have subdued my days of unremitting adventure, but as luck would have it (careful what you wish for) a family relative engineered an opportunity for me on the Alaska oil pipeline. In 1975, he was one of a hundred oil executives seeking to hire young men for the over-the-top pay scales rendered for employees of the Alyeska Pipeline Company. I was enlisted as a 'welder's helper,' at fifteen dollars an hour plus overtime, and was involved in constructing the above-ground pipeline from the Arctic Ocean, at Pump Station One, winding a hundred miles due south over the treeless tundra to the Brooks Range of Alaska.

My summer stretch on the pipeline project was rugged but also an immeasurable education about life beyond academia. I quickly learned that Oklahoma welders were not the open-minded, worldly-educated, university-types seeking adventure like a new graduate straight out of college. I shortly appreciated it was best to keep my opinions and assertions to myself. They were a rough crew assembled in the uninhabited North, and knife fights would suddenly break out in the camp supper line over the smallest affronts. I was a union member only for that summer.

After my return home from the pipeline project, my father mentioned to me a career in stock brokerage. I was surprised at his suggestion as I had no clue about stocks or bonds. Yet again, a relative of ours at a leading financial company—Paine, Webber, Jackson & Curtis—found a branch manager in Roanoke, Virginia, to take me on as a trainee. After training in the "Star City of the South," I soon moved to the Washington D.C. office where I became knowledgeable and adept at all the firm's product offerings. After several years, and during a time when President Reagan was shot by John Hinckley Jr. not far from our office, I decided to move to Wall Street to further my career. A broker/dealer institutional trading firm in mid-town Manhattan hired me as an associate. Besides learning under the principals of that firm, it was my father and his two partners, Gibb Kane and Harry Burn, who mentored me during the 1980s. New York is where I gained the business acumen and workings of Wall Street.

By the early 1990s, Dad and I found ourselves together again in Palm Beach, Florida. Dad had retired from his firm in Connecticut and I had left the hectic life of New York City. We lived in his condominium overlooking the ocean, on US Route 1, known as South Ocean Boulevard. It was there, during the recessionary years of 1991 and 1992, that we began thinking of investment opportunities outside of the US (we were not optimistic about the outlook for gaining US stock market appreciation, as US households were mired in deep financial distress; we even wrote a book about our concerns called *The Debt Penalty)*. When Dad attended a London conference on the subject of country funds—listed funds of single country, blue-chip stocks—he hatched an idea. On returning to Florida, he announced we were going to take a trip to the Far East. The great adventure had begun.

CHAPTER 2

ARRIVAL IN HONG KONG

I awoke disoriented and confused. There were people all around me, faces I didn't know, and we were being pitched sideways in our seats. For a moment we were held in a state of limbo, falling to the right. I turned to glance over my shoulder. Through the rows of portals, I looked down on brightly lit buildings, their chockablock formations reached ominously toward us like tentacles from a massive sea creature. I sucked in my breath. We were flying awfully low over Hong Kong harbor's Kowloon district, engine noise throughout the cabin deafening, and I watched as the wingtip brushed close to the concrete high rises. Suddenly, we righted ourselves, leveling against the night, and the 747 touched down onto the runway at the Kai Tak International Airport.

Nearly twenty hours of travel passing over the Pacific Ocean and we'd entered a new land.

I exhaled.

It was April 1992. My father and I were back for our second visit to Asia and to what was becoming our second home. In February, we had spent two weeks at the famous Peninsula Hotel meeting with numerous business leaders, getting an inside view of what was actually happening in the Greater China region. The 1989 Tiananmen Square crackdown was still a fresh topic, although most explanations we heard were different than Western media reports. The clampdown was viewed as an unfortunate event but not a reversal in China's economic revival.

The Tiananmen Square incident didn't help with the growing fears of the pending 1997 handover of Hong Kong by the British back to China. But if those fears were unfounded, then the extreme low valuations of the Hong Kong stock market might truly be a bargain investment. We decided to set up an investment firm to take advantage of the opportunity we saw developing, invest our own money, and get a better feel for the various market mechanics and idiosyncrasies in the stock market. Then we'd spread our thoughts to investors in the US before the handover.

Now, back in the city, I began the task of figuring out how to establish our discretionary investment management company. The effort entailed creating a new Hong Kong limited company which would be registered and properly licensed with the securities regulators. The new company would also provide the necessary work visas for both my father and me to be managing from Hong Kong.

Issuing work visas from a company not yet established was something the Hong Kong immigration department had great difficulty understanding.

"Mr. McConnell," the man at immigration said, "how do you seek work visas through a company that is not real?"

"It will be real, that's the point," I countered. "The new company will employ us and local employees as well."

"There is no company now!"

"That's why I'm here, to set up the brand-new company." I looked around the immigration facilities. "In fact, I want to set it up here through this very department." Our company secretary had furnished all the articles of incorporation and background forms needed for the department to recognize our company and to issue proper work visas.

"You cannot get work visa from company that is not real."

"It will be real."

Around and around we went like a carousel without end, me doing my best to explain, and the immigration officials insistently questioning why two expatriates were seeking work visas from a company that didn't exist. I felt discouragement wash through me like a wave. The granting of work visas from a non-operating company was just not any procedure in the immigration department's manuals. Financial firms in Hong Kong, mainly British institutions, sponsored the hiring and employing of workers.

Concurrent to this discussion, the officials in charge of our application kept asking for more and more details and documentation on both of us, even insisting on getting a certificate of my father's 1946 graduation from Princeton University. I wondered if they'd want to see library cards and track our reading habits, or maybe speak with old flames. They seemed almost desperate to know where we came from and what brought us here. I can't blame them, but we went back and forth like this for weeks.

Eventually we prevailed. Things happen like that. If you're persistent enough, others gradually begin to understand your motives and find a place for them in their frame of reference. Change in protocol takes time. Luckily, they never found out I was harboring images of becoming the next Tai Pan of the Noble House—a Dirk Struan of the investment community. I'm pretty sure they would have laughed me out of town.

Our employment visas were granted and we went about trying to register our company with the Hong Kong Securities and Futures Commission (SFC). When a well-known law firm in the city said they'd help us for twenty-thousand US dollars, I decided to do it myself. My father was personally funding all aspects of our new venture in Hong Kong and we had to find ways to exist without going broke. It was another long process, filling out forms and answering questions hundreds of times. But each turning of the sun across the fragrant harbor moved us closer to our goal. Over the course of the next weeks, the city revealed its mysteries to me like a hedge maze: a disorienting amalgam of streets and channels came upon me and fell away. I'd stumble upon parades and night markets; uncover new ways to communicate, mixing broken English with body movements and gestures like an amateur mime in a foreign land. I held up my hands to an invisible glass box and moved my fingers against its smooth surface. People looked at me with quizzical expressions, passed by me on all sides. The glass felt firm against my palms but the air coming off the sea rushed through my outstretched fingers. Ships trudged through the port, modern containers setting out next to oriental sails. Bicyclists and rickshaw drivers swerved around me. I stood there moving my arms about in the air, this side of the box, then that, feeling for an edge or a frame. A boy pointed at me while walking with his mother. The mother looked, smiled, and moved them along. Cars and trams whizzed by, honking vigorously. Then just like that I found the door, pushed it open, and stepped through. Our company was becoming real.

With registration almost taken care of, it was time for a name. My father's former firm had moved from New York City to Cos Cob, Connecticut, which ran along the shores of the Long Island Sound. They decided to name the firm after the street address and came up with Sound Shore Management. It had a safe sounding ring to it for an investment firm. When we began developing our Far East investment company, we were then living on South Ocean Boulevard in Palm Beach, Florida, and were moving to the south seas of China, hence the name South Ocean Management evolved. It was a well thought of name in Chinese as well (南海管理有限公司).

At the end of all our various registration processes, I set out to find and enlist a locally-based custodian bank for our investment program. Because we had met and developed relationships with many local securities brokers and research analysts in the city, we wanted to be able to remunerate these trusted agents with our commission business for their continued research and support. We would need a custodian arrangement for our client accounts to trade and settle stock transactions with the various brokers we intended to use.

This was not an uncommon arrangement for independent investment firms to operate. But finding a custodian bank to hold and entrust our client accounts was another story. I started calling around to big, brand name institutions, asking to come by and talk about a custodial relationship. Many of these banks were initially eager and positive, gladly inviting me to meet and discuss our program with them. Yet after many sessions and discussions, they all decided we were not eligible for a custodial arrangement. No further reasons were given for declining our request.

After weeks of searching, it wasn't until we were directed to the Bank of Bermuda where we succeeded in finding a banking custodian. As a rule, we found out, the big banks only accepted large institutional accounts as clients. Why those brand name bankers couldn't explain that to us initially, in my days of investigating, is beyond me. It was many years later, in 2004, that HSBC Group acquired the Bank of

Bermuda, which became the focus for its fund management and private banking activities.

We organized our investment process whereby each client could have their own portfolios managed separately by South Ocean. My Dad wanted to manage segregated accounts as he did with his former US investment firm, and those accounts could be offered custody arrangements with the Bank of Bermuda as well. South Ocean would regularly produce individual portfolio month-end reports, including important information such as performance updates and analysis.

To produce these reports, the issue was how to account for performance in dual currencies. We were to report results in US dollars from investments made in Hong Kong dollars. In the early nineties there was no off-the-shelf accounting software available that would account for currency translations. Only custom, large scale, institutional software programs were available to create those kinds of reports.

To explain the currency translation dilemma a bit further, when we invested portfolio cash into Hong Kong dollar denominated common shares, we were investing in the local currency of Hong Kong dollars. Yet when we reported the month-end values in US dollars, we needed to translate returns and performance from local currency (i.e. Hong Kong dollars) into US dollar equivalent amounts.

At that time, the US was the most advanced country in software reporting solutions for the financial industry. There were many desktop portfolio management accounting systems available, but they only reported in US dollars. Currency translation accounting systems essentially ran on giant, back office mainframe computers. The desktop solutions we needed to run in-house were not readily available on the market.

During my career in New York, I had analyzed and found several excellent portfolio accounting systems that worked well and I helped implement an efficient system for the firm's accounting and reporting purposes. In Hong Kong, though, I was challenged with this currency translation issue.

One accounting software company in California claimed they did have a system that could be run on a personal desktop computer and also report currency translation. Yet, even after spending three days at their home offices, back-testing their own system, I determined their claims were mistaken. I tried working another PC-based software program recommended to me, unfortunately, the British accounting program also proved very complex and inefficient. I spent five intensive months working that system before determining it too was not practicable to smoothly run our operating and reporting requirements.

By this time, my father was getting impatient. He couldn't understand why there was no desktop computer solution to do the job of managing segregated accounts and reporting performance on each. If I could have easily gone out and found one at the local computer supply store, I would have. Then, I came across an interesting system in use at the Bank of Canada and delved deeply into its workings. After months of analysis, and years of several failed systems, I finally recommended the program to our board of directors.

This substantial, complex program, was called Portia. It met many CFA-required parameters of reporting and was the only system we could operate using a desktop PC. Priced at a cost of about US$50,000, Portia was not a small sum to invest, and I was the only one who had any knowledge of whether it would work. Dad and South Ocean's shareholders practically held a gun to my head after they agreed to buy and implement the system on my recommendation. They made it clear it had better work.

Portia worked as expected. At that time, no investment management firm in Hong Kong had such a comprehensive accounting system. Most fund managers used a single pooled fund for their clients to invest and would simply calculate a net asset value (NAV) of the pooled fund, using that calculation to report to clients. NAV reporting, though, is not a concise attribution and is deficient in several areas of true performance reporting. Still, that was the primary scheme of reporting used by portfolio managers in Hong Kong in the nineties (other than mainframe computer systems at large, institutional offshore banks).

Several years after successfully operating the system, the Bank of Bermuda lawyers gave me a call. They had specific questions about how we used it. Soon afterwards they were using Portia throughout their organization as the primary reporting system to clients. After HSBC's later acquisition of the Bank of Bermuda, HSBC continued reporting to all its custody accounts using the Portia system as well.

• • •

In those early days, things in Hong Kong progressed rapidly. South Ocean Management was off and running and occasionally I'd take a moment to look out over the city and breathe. From Vermont to Alaska to Hong Kong; all one big adventure. Once you start out on something, pieces fall into place, you begin to feel more at ease. You make it work, no matter the obstacles. You may even find a home halfway around the world where you least expected.

But I never did get over those breath-taking Kai Tak landings.

CHAPTER 3

THE AMAZING FAX MACHINE

In our initial months of launching South Ocean Management as a Hong Kong investment firm, we began operating out of our leased, two-bedroom flat on the forty-eighth floor overlooking Victoria Harbor. The Marriott's Atrium was decorated with luxurious marbled floors and expensive wood paneled walls. The top floors of the hotel were segregated from the main hotel and designated only for long-term rental clientele. On various trips over the next two years, Dad and I operated from this vantage point in Hong Kong.

At the time of our arrival, the city skyline was lined with construction cranes, like giant birds standing erect on the horizon. Property development in both commercial and residential real estate was booming, and public infrastructure projects were on the rise. A mega landfill dredging operation across the harbor was just beginning. We watched the giant sprayer suck up the bottom of the harbor and spew it out to fill in the expanding shoreline. The workers also carried dirt on additional barges and sprayed it like the arc from a fire hose into the air, working round the clock continuously for a number of months during our stay. I liked watching the land take shape far below.

Today, that reclaimed land of West Kowloon is completed and bears underground trains, tunnels, highways, and multi-towered office and residential buildings. The posh Ritz-Carlton Hotel occupies the top floors of Hong Kong's highest skyscraper, with stunning surrounding views of Kowloon and across the harbor to mountainous Hong Kong Island. Rising 484 meters (1,588 ft), the ICC (International Commerce Centre) is the tallest building in Hong Kong as well as the ninth tallest building in the world. All built atop reclaimed harbor. Hong Kong's rapid urban development was grand, modern, and extremely efficient at utilizing every square foot of space.

In our early days, Hong Kong's long-term economic development continued unabated by the past concerns of neighboring China and the many unknowns facing the future of the island. The Basic Law, negotiated by Britain and China and signed by China in April 1990, allowed Hong Kong to operate as a Separate Administrative Region (SAR) under a "one country, two systems" jurisdiction of China for fifty years after the Handover in 1997. As a general rule, most Hong Kong residents carried second passports, just in case the Beijing Chinese government had ulterior plans for Hong Kong other than abiding the rules established under the Basic Law.

The big question on everybody's mind was whether or not China was bent on confiscating all assets in Hong Kong after the 1997 Handover. But if so, why were these huge public and private projects going forward? The grandiose economic infrastructure projects being initiated were certainly not the undertakings of the British establishment (who would be leaving after June of 1997), but of the new and powerful Hong Kong Chinese families and institutions.

These politicians and developers were full steam-ahead and damn the torpedoes. The local businessmen and government officials certainly knew better than any outside observers what would happen to Hong Kong.

The real fears of China's eventual rule over Hong Kong were most evident in the Hong Kong stock market. Not long before the July Handover, the Hang Seng Index sold at just under fifteen times earnings while most other Asian markets—including Singapore, Taiwan and Malaysia—all sold at greater than twenty times earnings.

Hong Kong stocks sold at much steeper discounts than other Asian stocks, especially the smaller, newly listed industrial companies. With long histories of business dealings with Western customers and markets, Hong Kong companies were arguably more adept than their Asian neighbors and in a better position to serve international markets. These experienced companies were transferring their high cost Hong Kong operations across the border, setting up factories in southern China, and enjoying expanding margins. Additionally, there was the eventual promise of expanding business into China's own fast-growing economic progress. These dynamics were all significant considerations that were simply ignored or not appreciated by public equity investors. Even the potential and remote notion that China might actually partner with Hong Kong companies in business, rather than be a perceived totalitarian adversary, was diametrically opposite to the prevailing attitudes and opinions of most investors.

Our convictions, in the face of this pessimism, rose from being there on-the-ground and conducting our own examinations and analysis. We believed the threat of China taking over Hong Kong was actually an opportunity and we outlined our reasoning in a book titled *The Investment Opportunity of a Lifetime: Hong Kong 1997 and Beyond*. Much of what we expected for the future of Hong Kong and

China remains relevant today, as does the primary philosophy and basis by which we view our investment program—that is, owning well-managed, solid businesses listed in Hong Kong of companies benefiting from operations growing in China.

While gaining these insightful conclusions, we continued to build our investment firm, furnishing our office/flat with some basic equipment. I had a small but heavy, somewhat primitive, laptop tethered to a wall socket and printer. Dad would often use the business center downstairs for typing his letters. As email had not yet evolved, the fax machine was our key communication and marketing tool.

We used the fax endlessly. Not only were we sending faxes across the globe, keeping in touch with clients and our advisors in the US, but also locally. Hong Kong was fax-crazed. If we called a company headquarters or broker to ask for a meeting, we were asked to first send a fax. If we needed more pens and paper from the office supply store across the street, they asked for a fax. Sometimes, even restaurants wanted a fax to confirm reservations.

Operating a fax was tedious and often exasperating. First writing and printing out a Word document or handwritten letter, arranging the pages carefully for transmission, and then dialing in the chosen fax number. Once the contraption connected to the number dialed (with a loud, high-pitched squeal), you would literally stand over the machine praying the pages inserted didn't crumble going through. Remarkably, the fax machine then sent audio-frequency tones over the telephone wires, half-way around the globe, and wonderfully reconstructed the text at the other end where our message would be printed out.

Those were the meticulous operating procedures needed for the fax. Each night, before retiring, Dad and I would remind each other to check the paper scroll and replenish it in case it ran out in the middle of an important overnight message.

Today, those efforts seem an unambiguously primitive and clumsy means of communicating. The manual efforts of running a fax stand in stark contrast to today's click/send world of email, where we seldom give a second thought to its operation. This is a vast improvement in such a relatively short period of time.

In those early days, before the advent of cheap Voice over Internet Protocol technology, making an overseas call was prohibitively expensive. Fax communications were less expensive but were only completed with long, type-written, concise messages. Though a time-consuming effort, without the facsimile, we would not have been able to function. It was a vital device and essential to the development and running of our operations.

As Nicholas Negroponte forecast in his 1995 best seller, *Being Digital*, the digital information world would soon grow exponentially. He likened digital advancement to compounding:

> The change from atoms to bits is irrevocable and unstoppable.
>
> Why now? Because the change is also exponential—small differences of yesterday can have suddenly *shocking consequences* tomorrow.
>
> Did you ever know the childhood conundrum of working for a penny a day for a month, but doubling your salary each day? If you started this wonderful pay scheme on New Year's Day, you would be earning more than $10 million per day on the last day of January. This is the part most people remember. What we do not realize is that, using the same scheme, we would earn only about $13 million if January were three days shorter… when an effect is exponential, those last three days mean a lot! We are approaching those last *three days* in the spread of computing and digital telecommunications. [italics added]

What a forecast that turned out to be. Looking back at the drudgery of communicating by fax when first starting South Ocean to today's convenience of interacting over the internet is astounding. It's quite remarkable, and unimaginable just a few years back, the levels of productivity gains we've reached in a very short period of time. Can you recall the first mobile phones—the size of a brick, which, at that time in the late 1980s, was an enormous, untethered advancement to the landline phone?

This advent of rapid technological improvements is a prime illustration of how China has accelerated from a backwater, inward-looking country to the world's second largest economy and powerhouse today.

Digital technology was driving China's dynamic progress. The evolutionary transformation was happening rapidly. When we first traveled into mainland China in the early '90s, there were no conveniences for ordinary citizens. There were no landline telephones in homes nor any public phone booths on street corners. Bicycles were the prime means of transportation and Shanghai streets were a sea of bicycles. Today, the city is a parking lot of cars traveling on new ring roads. There are twice as many internet and cellular phone users in China than in the US.

Naysayers in the late '90s believed the Chinese people would never adapt to buying goods or services online. Chinese were overly suspicious, they contended, and unlikely to buy any item they couldn't tangibly touch. Ecommerce giant, Alibaba, was founded in 1999, just twenty years ago. Alibaba's Singles Day event in November last year hit $30.8 billion in sales over a 24-hour period, and most of those transactions were over a hand-held cellular device. Buying a meal at a KFC or Starbucks (both of which were just being introduced to the mainland when we arrived) is with a digital wallet on a mobile phone application. The accelerating gains from 'digital' transformation throughout the PRC—including leading edge advancements in artificial intelligence, engineering, robotics, biomedicines, quantum computing to name a few—are testament to the Middle Kingdom's astonishing rise and advancement.

Unencumbered by the IT legacy constraints endured in the West, China is setting the stage for 'shocking consequences' as Negroponte attested. Where will China be in the last three days of its 'digital' progress?

From our top floor perch at the Marriott Atrium, we were witnessing firsthand the phenomenal, phoenix-like rise of China. During an early trip with a Hong Kong financier to Guangdong Province, we became further convinced of our contention to follow the local Hong Kong entrepreneurs into developing China.

Our financier friend Peter, invited us along to meet the head Provincial governmental official of Guangdong, a province just north of Hong Kong with eighty million permanent residents and another thirty million migrant inhabitants. We entered an old, run-down administrative building in an unassuming neighborhood just on the outskirts of the capital city of Guangdong Province, and continued upstairs to a cramped, un-airconditioned room where this official sat at a small metal desk in a short-sleeved white shirt. He could have been mistaken for any one of an army of accountants in some tax department. Yet, Peter told us he was one of the more powerful men in southern China. He didn't speak English, but he was friendly, good-natured, and cordial. Dad and I listened silently.

While I was sitting there, a thought struck me: this was a communist! My first encounter with America's nemesis and not at all as I had imagined he might be. I'd even enjoy hanging out and having a beer with him. Back then, Pabst Blue Ribbon was the biggest selling beer on the mainland, brewed in Guangdong Province. In contrast to the US positioning of Pabst as the blue-collar drinker's favorite, China Pabst Blue Ribbon Beer, or Lán dài píjiǔ, was a luxury brand and very expensive.

Peter would occasionally translate for us. He had returned with Dad and me to talk with the official (after many previous visits, entertaining at late-night karaoke soirées and gaining a *guanxi* relationship) about a development project he wanted to pursue along the Pearl River, south of Guangzhou. When we left the official's office, we traveled by car through small villages to a cul-de-sac next to the Pearl River. It was Peter's idea to build a boat and barge dock nearby and develop a logistics shipping center. We exited the car and began walking along a hillside dike above the river when Peter looked down to some newly tilled soil. Evidently, a local farmer had been working the small plot.

"I've got to do something about that right away," he said and pointed down to the new plantings. "If I want to lease the land along the river for this project I have to make payment amends towards any peasants occupying the land. The locals probably saw me visit here last time and figured I was seeking to develop, then came out here and planted this unused area with some vegetables to extract compensation."

Nuances such as this meant it was wise and advantageous to follow the local Hong Kong investors. How could any unsuspecting Westerner foresee the many snares?

But even for the locals, it wasn't easy doing business on the Mainland. Nor was it easy for expat Americans to do business in the British Crown Colony of Hong Kong—even with the amazing fax machine.

CHAPTER 4

DEVELOPMENT OF OUR INVESTMENT THESIS

Our philosophical views were forming contrary to the predominant opinions expressed on TV and the English-written newspapers, including the local South China Morning Post. With our unaccustomed, foreigner viewpoint we could see where the West failed to recognize China's successes because it focused predominantly on China's violations of human rights. The Tiananmen Square incident was recent and this failure far outweighed the progressions and successes in other areas. The overnight rising standard of living in China was one of the greater accomplishments in any country's history, and that progress was just beginning. China was encouraging foreign investment and free enterprise on the mainland. Businessmen and tourists were being welcomed as China opened up its former closed system and prohibitively restrictive practices.

Future growth was also not impeded by a list of social problems, such as drug abuse, illegitimacy, and AIDS, which were costly problems in the West. Racial and religious tensions were mostly absent in China and thus terrorism was not an issue. The Chinese were savers, saving at ten times the rate of savings in the US. Debt loads for Chinese citizens were minimal. The same migratory transitions that took place in the United States more than a hundred years ago are a powerful illustration of the forces driving China's trapped rural population—over nine hundred million farmers seeking a better life. Hundreds of millions of young Chinese moving from the farms to cities, willing to work and improve their lots. In the West, the opposite trends were in force: aging, retiring citizens moving out of crime-ridden cities to seek country homes and live off sometimes meager pensions.

My father and I watched the events unfold. There were continuous mainstream media prognostications during the run-up to the Handover that the tiny island state of Hong Kong was doomed and destined to become a second-rate city of China. Images were painted of massive crackdowns on the Hong Kong people and its institutions when China was to take back the territory after July 1, 1997. But the deleterious suggestions that China would use a ruthless and authoritarian hand, with intentions bent on driving out all the "capitalists" and detractors from the island, were not based on evidence we were encountering. Hong Kong was too important to China's long-term plans. Besides being viewed as the Monaco of the East, with The Peak residential area at the top of Hong Kong island seen as the epitome of ultimate success, Hong Kong was the largest foreign direct investor into the motherland, funding much needed improvements for China's impoverished conditions. If it were shown by the Chinese authorities that they gave Hong Kong full autonomous rule and abided the Basic Law agreements, then it would certainly set an example that 'renegade' Taiwan was under no imminent threat by the PRC. I believe the authorities silently contemplated that Hong Kong's largest banking institute, Hongkong and Shanghai Banking Corporation (now HSBC), was also too important for its future plans. As an offshore lending institute, the bank was a link to the world's trading systems (it was also an opportune first stop destination for any cadre needing an offshore banking depository for his questionable monetary gains). These factors would be heedless to ignore. Hong Kong had too much to offer and China wasn't going to kill its golden goose.

As ludicrous as those dire predictions seem today, they were widely disseminated in the press and routinely backed up, time and time again, with mention of the 1989 Tiananmen Square crackdown. By the Handover, most Chinese citizens I met on the Mainland had gotten over the Tiananmen crackdown and were focused on making a better life for themselves. But CNN's Beijing correspondent, Mike Chinoy—even fifteen years after the event—rarely finished his television commentary without some mention of Tiananmen Square. Though he couldn't help but recognize the incredible improvement of life that was happening before him in Beijing, he could never admit this was happening in the absence of an open government.

The repetitive, prejudiced views of Hong Kong's future, we believed, were unfounded and biased. The prevailing belief suggested the leaders in Beijing would not honor their promise under the Joint Declaration with Britain to maintain "one country two systems." This outlook made our contrarian speculation even more enticing.

I commented once to a journalist in Asia that his colleagues always report the negative angles in stories. He told me: "Our headlines rarely blare good news, but the fact is we have to sell newspapers." (Why it's so prevalent that humans find negative, catastrophic news more worthy than in-depth, balanced reporting is another issue, but it can create opportunities for informed analysts).

Headlines often portrayed potential conflict and widespread chaos for Hong Kong after the Handover, even when there was no substantial backing or substance for those contentions. This news reporting was the prevailing sentiment being expressed almost daily, which, in turn, made investors nervous.

Amidst such an overwhelming perspective, we began formulating our initial philosophy to own depressed Hong Kong equities that were benefiting from China's growth. We believed the post-Handover period would prove that Hong Kong would continue to operate as before and once that notion was believed by investors, depressed valuations in the Hong Kong market would rifle upwards.

We doubted the adverse outlook and believed there would be no interference from China in Hong Kong's affairs. Not only was Hong Kong a cheap stock market, but the potential opportunities beyond the Handover were massive. It didn't escape our attention that, in reality, if China really wanted to oust everyone and loot the island's wealth, they could do so at any time without ever firing a shot just by turning off the only fresh water supply to Hong Kong (piped in from a large reservoir located just north in Guangdong Province, China).

It was clear to me that China's non-democratically elected government was not the main issue challenging most Chinese citizens. For mainland peoples, getting ahead with better living conditions was the prime objective.

We were not deterred in moving forward with our plans. South Ocean's program would operate as an institutional investment money management company fashioned along the same operating principles as Dad's previous investment firm in Connecticut. Every US institutional client would receive monthly statements, quarterly analysis, and yearly visits by phone or in person, just as they were served by US managers. The investing doctrine would be long term, whereby our intentions were to hold—for over a year—stocks that we believed were cheap and would provide excess returns from holding long term.

We were not proposing a scattered, pan-Asia portfolio offering either (which many Asian managers promised). All our focus was on the singularly dynamic outlook we saw developing within China. We never designed a geographically Asian diversified portfolio of stocks because after traveling the region and meeting many analysts we were convinced that all roads led to China. No other country held as much promise nor immense depth. Most Southeast Asian economies were dominated by ethnic Chinese people anyway. These expatriates were likely beholden to their homeland, in one form or another, and China would always benefit from all of these countrymen intertwining their country's progress with that of China.

Our investment program would serve each account similarly as our investment philosophy and processes were unlikely to change with the trends we saw developing. We would remain steadfast to the long-term premise that China would most likely continue its economic ascent out of socialistic restraints. This mandate would hold true throughout, regardless of any short-term, non-recurring events or market gyrations. We established this modus operandum at the beginning, but also added if any of our viewpoints or analysis were to change over the course of time, we would communicate them to our investors, allowing each account to reconsider their investments with us.

Our plan was to introduce and present our beliefs and opinions to the many CEOs and pension trustees Dad had known from his former Wall Street days. In the financial corridors around the US, as we trooped from one office to another, we visited with pension officers and trustees of large institutions. But we found we were actually receiving most of our initial interest from individual investors.

After making our presentation, we were often met with a response akin to: "McConnells, we like this story very much, but our investment mandate requires established track records before we can invest with South Ocean. Come back in three years. But could you possibly run my own account until then?"

Our focus was managing segregated institutional accounts but as we encountered personal interest from many of those who heard of our mission, we asked ourselves, could we find a way to incorporate smaller sized accounts? After all, we were investing our own money so why not the investable capital of our friends? It wouldn't be possible, though, to manage a myriad of individual accounts at different brokerages and banks. We needed one account to offer that we could manage efficiently.

We decided in early 1993 to form a Delaware limited partnership, appropriately named Hong Kong Partners LP, for both institutional and non-institutional clients. This would allow our friends to join our investment program and benefit alongside our large investors.

A US-domiciled limited partnership would have several advantages for individuals. Each limited partner in the fund would have their own capital account with each individually accounted for and invested alongside all of our accounts. The fund's portfolio would be run on a parallel basis with all other accounts and thereby share similar results. In other words, buys and sales in the fund would be on the same percentage basis as we administered for the main accounts. If we decided, for instance, to initiate a 3% portfolio purchase in a particular stock, the fund would also be buying a 3% position alongside all other managed accounts (3% of total portfolio value).

Another advantage came from a tax angle, especially beneficial for individual taxpayers. For example, on January 1, the fund initiated a purchase of XYZ stock at $10.00 per share. Later that year, on June 30, a new investor (Mr. Webber) makes an initial investment in the fund. At that time, XYZ stock owned in the portfolio has gone up and is valued at $20.00 per share. On December 1 that year, the fund sells XYZ stock at $30, resulting in a $20.00 per share capital gain from the initial purchase price. Mr. Webber's gain will be recognized as $10.00 per share, from his cost basis on June 30, and reported on his year-end K1 tax form which the fund produced yearly. This tax accounting is not available in a mutual fund whereby a realized long-term capital gain may have an adverse tax consequence for a late investor. The investor in a mutual fund may be hit with a large tax of which he had little or no gain.

By the launch of the fund in July 1993, two dozen limited partners decided to join us—mostly successful, self-made individuals and entrepreneurs, Wall Street financial professionals, college endowment trustees, and individual pension officers.

We were quite unique in our approach to handling accounts in Hong Kong. South Ocean was a Hong Kong-domiciled management company, operating in Hong Kong under Hong Kong laws and taxation. Most investment management firms in Hong Kong were incorporated off-shore, a guised way to avoid paying Hong Kong taxes even though they had offices and day-to-day operations in Hong Kong. We were adamant on dispelling any perception that South Ocean was some waystation incorporated overseas, primarily organized to avoid taxes. South Ocean Management, Ltd. would operate under Hong Kong's tax regime and be responsible for full taxes on its earnings (which were relatively low anyway as Hong Kong corporate tax rates are only 15%).

Second, most management firms operating in Hong Kong offered only corporate fund set-ups for their investors, commonly Bermuda or Cayman Island corporate entities. A few firms offered private Master Limited Partnership formats, but South Ocean's US clients, through the Delaware limited partnership arrangement, would be indisputably recognized as invested in a legitimate, flow-through US taxable entity. Each US resident would be responsible for filing their K1 partnership tax returns furnished at year-end. As an onshore, Delaware entity, limited partners in the fund would not be obliged to partake in all the complexities and questions involved with offshore investment platforms.

Non-US investors would also be eligible to invest in the partnership, with their separate capital accounts not subject to any US assessments. We offered one Delaware Limited Partnership for both domestic and foreign investors and without the needed structure for a private Master Limited Partnership set-up with a foreign domicile.

Fortunately, Hong Kong Partners LP began trading just when the Hong Kong market was rising sharply.

CHAPTER 5

SOUTH OCEAN'S INVESTMENT PROGRAM

Our timing with the launch of our Delaware Limited Partnership—Hong Kong Partners LP—in 1993 was fortuitous in that there was high exuberance bubbling in Hong Kong's stock market. Barton Biggs, Chairman of Morgan Stanley Investment Management, pronounced after a visit to mainland China, "I'm tuned in, overfed, and maximum bullish." Biggs was well respected and had many followers on Wall Street at the time.

The Morgan Stanley call had a major effect on the Hong Kong market. 'Hot' money flows from the U.S. were coming ashore, even though at that time China seemed a shaky bet. Biggs was not oblivious to the risks of emerging markets, but he was a firm believer in the long-term value of China.

In the second half of 1993, the large cap Hang Seng Index (a weighted index used to record and monitor daily changes of the largest companies of the Hong Kong stock market) garnered much of the money inflows and propelled the Index dramatically higher. It rose from 7,099 to 11, 888—4,800 points, gaining 67.5% and breaking through the 10,000 level for the first time in December of that year. These were heady times.

The main index's primary targets were property developer Cheung Kong, ports and property developer Hutchison Whampoa, and Hong Kong's largest mortgage lender, HSBC (then known as Hongkong and Shanghai Banking Corporation). Cheung Kong's stock gained 77.6% in the second half rally, HSBC was up 56.4%, and Hutchison Whampoa rose 84.7%. Striking gains in just the last six months of that year!

Though the Hang Seng Index was considered the main indicator of the overall market performance in Hong Kong, there was actually a vast dichotomy in the performance of the hundreds of secondary-listed smaller stocks not represented in the blue-chip index. The momentum of foreign money flows, enthusiastically following Morgan Stanley's lead, were primarily buying into the larger, liquid Hang Seng Index constituent stocks. In all the excitement, even local investors were joining the fray, buying what was moving and ignoring most other areas of the market. Smaller stocks, for the most part, did not partake in the dramatic rise of the large cap index stocks until late in the rally.

Yet, during the stock market's rise in 1993, a large question mark started brewing in Hong Kong. Chris Patton, Britain's last appointed governor of Hong Kong before the Handover, was making controversial calls for more democracy—visibly seeking to become Prime Minister of England after his Hong Kong stint. His statements infuriated China. China saw it as tampering with the Joint Declaration, inscribed between the two countries in 1984, guaranteeing Hong Kong's social and economic systems for fifty years after the Handover. China was calling Patton all sorts of names. The row caused deep suspicions and divisions between Britain and China. Hong Kong was right in the middle of the fracas.

By early 1994, China-bull Biggs suddenly withdrew his enthusiastic call on Hong Kong, and foreign money quickly sold out. Stock prices began declining swiftly. The ensuing few months witnessed a steep decline in the major index, from a high on January 4 of 12,201 to a low of 8,412 on May 5. The Hang Seng, which had risen rapidly six months before, was down 31% in the first four months of 1994. Smaller, less liquid stocks were even more volatile, as the exuberant but brief excitement in 1993 evaporated and the mood turned despondent. Stocks became depressed in the relentless selling and remained low for several years. Less liquid stocks were battered with the onslaught. Hong Kong's stock market wouldn't break above the 12,000 mark again until late 1996.

Once again, China was being viewed with a skeptical eye. Concurrent to the quarrel between Patton and China, rapid growth of China's transitory economy was suddenly attended by a concerning rise in inflation. Since the 1978 reforms, China's economy was growing an average 9% a year, and consumer prices were held mostly steady (inflation, as measured by the consumer price index, was running in the single digits). Then in 1994, prices abruptly started rising over 20%, especially in the sensitive food sectors. Policymakers were alarmed because food was a large household expenditure and residents' resentment grew.

Though China had devalued its currency in early 1994, raising the exchange rate from 5.6 to 8.7 yuan per dollar, devaluation was not the major cause for the surge in inflation (rather, long held centrally planned underpricing of consumer goods, especially of food commodities, was the culprit). The country's central banker, Zhu Rongji, head of the People's Bank of China, began a nationwide campaign against inflation, cooling down the economy by lowering the economic growth rate. He declared an austerity program of immense proportions that successfully led to price stability and continued growth for China in the years thereafter. That accomplishment greatly aided the PRC's advancement, and China would also be commended during the 1997 Asian Financial Crisis for keeping its currency stable when all other Asian countries experienced huge devaluations.

From 1994 through 1996, Hong Kong's stock market was volatile. This was also a period where the imminent death of China's leader Deng Xiaoping was routinely mentioned in the press, then to be later denied by China. But each announcement sent Hong Kong stocks reeling. Weekly headlines of Deng's declining health frightened investors and brought on more uncertainty. When the official announcement of Deng's passing did finally come to pass in early 1997, stocks had already dropped so many times before that the market actually rose that day, closing up four hundred points.

Hong Kong's stock market was still in its infancy in the early nineties. When we arrived, the total market capitalization of the main index was only $160 billion. Today, the Hang Seng has increased to over US$2 trillion. Free float market capitalization, or shares not held by insiders, was much smaller in that time than total market capitalization. Therefore, relatively small buying or selling programs would accentuate moves considerably.

Hong Kong stocks were buffeted by many crosscurrents, and by early 1995 the volatility was getting rough for Dad, who was about to turn seventy. I took over as President and manager of the accounts. Dad would continue visiting Hong Kong frequently until 2000 but the one visit he wanted to attend, and didn't, was the July 1997 handover. Landlords and hotels were tripling prices of stays in Hong Kong to absurd levels. Even his cherished Ritz Carlton located in the

Central district wouldn't offer a long-time, favored client a reasonable price. Unfortunately, my apartment was just a one bedroom and had no extra room. Dad decided the trip from Florida was not worth it even though, in his eyes, it was the major turning point for the Hong Kong stock market. He reluctantly did not attend the ceremonies.

The handover was a very wet affair. Throughout the five days of ceremonies, rain drenched the island. I attended a party in a restaurant with a patio overlooking the harbor. On June 30, 1997, the British flag was taken down and handed to the departing governor, signaling an end to British rule. As the HMS Britannia sailed out of Victoria Harbor, with Prince Charles and Patton aboard, there was much emotion. There were many reactions from onlookers, but one of my colleagues dryly commented to me as we watched the ship sail away in the pouring rain, "That's the last of the Brits taking anything more out of Hong Kong." So much for weighty, teary-eyed sentiments. Hong Kong was in Chinese hands thereafter.

Many times, I have been asked what changes I've seen since the Handover. I can't say too many. Hong Kong continued to enjoy its busy, hectic ways and China wasn't interfering—at least to the levels feared by many commentators. For instance, on the day of the Handover, China's crack army units were to cross the border to be stationed on the island. A plethora of reporters traveled to the border to witness the soldiers crossing over. They were expecting tanks and artillery brigades with goose-stepping troops following, marching into the Territory, signaling the imminent Death of Hong Kong (that was also the cover title of the lead article of Fortune Magazine in 1995).

But the reporters, who had hoped to see some startling event while they waited in the rain, were disappointed and saddened. The army's covered truck convoys crossed into Hong Kong with no incident, drove unceremoniously to the barracks at the Prince of Wales building located on Hong Kong Island, and were never seen again.

My only glimpse of any Chinese army presence was walking past the entrance to the Prince of Wales building, where guards stood erect inside, rifles held in front, silent and motionless. The engraved wording on the wall of the building, which read Prince of Wales, though, had been scraped off. That title was no longer relevant and may have been the most noticeable change I witnessed.

One evening in the entertainment district of Lan Kwai Fong, I did see two army personnel, dressed in civilian clothes. My friend noticed them and pointed them out. They were just wandering, looking around and goggling at the famous party venue which was well known and of keen interest to many in China. The price of beer in Lan Kwai Fong establishments was not cheap, costing upwards of US$10 a pint. Those soldiers made wages of less than US$100 a month, or three dollars a day. That was probably a key point why we never saw the soldiers around town very often while off-duty.

Looking back at the early days of our Hong Kong adventure, it was clear many investors were too bullish on China and too simplistic in their perspective. China's opening its economy to the world has been measured, with fits and starts, and still proceeds today. By 2027, China will likely top the world in economic output. What will be interesting is what happens to Hong Kong after the first fifty years operating as a Special Administrative Region of China. In 2047, fifty years after the Hong Kong Handover, China will take full 'ownership' of Hong Kong, and perhaps promulgate its own laws rather than maintain Hong Kong's common law. This will be a monumental event.

CHAPTER 6

THE EARLY YEARS

By 1996, The Hong Kong stock market had grown to a total market capitalization of US$350 billion versus approximately $160 billion in 1992 when we arrived. The total number of listed companies had increased to 550 stocks. The Hong Kong Stock Exchange (HKSE) was just ten years old. The HKSE's 1986 founding was consummated by the merger of four different stock exchanges operating in Hong Kong. Prior to that, the stock market in Hong Kong was a loosely regulated affair. As far back as 1870, when the first 'companies' ordinance' was passed, stock trading worked outside on the sidewalks of Central (today's financial district). There were to be many speculative booms and collapses in market prices along the way, and by the 1970s, because of its colonial ties with Britain and common law system, Hong Kong had become a ranking Asian financial hub (outside of Japan).

In the 1980s, stock prices rose in Hong Kong almost in lockstep with the US markets. But with the 1987 Wall Street October Massacre, the Hong Kong markets were overwhelmed and unable to open for a week because of the influx of sell orders. A new regulatory body was established in May of 1989, the Securities and Futures Commission or SFC. The SFC was developed to oversee the Hong Kong Stock Exchange and bring about market discipline.

As confidence returned and grew with a more regulated stock exchange, many private trading companies, with long histories of business dealings with the West, began listing shares for public ownership. The listing requirements, though, would benefit and protect the founding families' ownership of their businesses as a minimum of only 25% of their companies was required to be offered to the public (minimum float). There were other listing requirements, but control would still remain in the hands of the founder shareholders. More often than not, investment bankers would bring the companies' initial public offerings at attractive low price-to-earnings ratios to increase investor interest.

Family controlled companies were viewed both positively and negatively. On the negative side, minority shareholders would have little say in how the companies were run. They would be subject to the whims of whatever the family decided to do. The founding families, it was often viewed, could benefit at the expense of minority shareholders.

We believed it favorable to invest alongside the listed family businesses, with some caveats. A family business that was listed on the HKSE would be required to report its financial records regularly. Since a Hong Kong family would not want to lose credibility in light of that revealing requirement, the controlling owners would seek to have their businesses well managed and further recognized as accomplished, successful enterprises (or lose 'face,' an unacceptable stigma in Chinese culture). Therefore, it was in the family's favor to better serve minority shareholders as well.

Ron Shaich, the founder and Chairman of Panera Bread, commented on founder-run companies: "Studies (such as this one from the Harvard Business Review) conclude that founder-led businesses often outperform professionally managed firms. I would suggest that they do so because the founder's commitment runs far deeper and is often longer-term in nature than that of the professional manager. And commitment and focus is what drives performance."[2]

Many of these smaller, growth companies with established track records and well-defined business plans, had, in our view, attractive qualities for our investment program. As those businesses and earnings grew, we envisioned that the low price-earnings multiples applied to the valuations would also expand. Many young companies we invested in during the nineties gave more than 100% returns due to the very fact they were cheap, undiscovered values when we started investing. Their earnings were growing and as the market capitalizations rose to thresholds where international, institutional investors could invest, the price-earnings multiples often expanded.

We wanted to initially buy those stocks where the price earnings ratio was half the expected growth rate. For example, if the next two years earnings growth was 20% annually, we didn't want to pay much more than ten times those expected earnings. I believe it was Benjamin Graham, the pioneer of investment analysis in the early 1900s, who stated a stock's price-earnings multiple should equate to the earnings growth rate of the company. A stock might not only rise with the 20% earnings growth, but also revalue upwards again with a higher price-earnings ratio. Graham, if he were alive back then, would have

---

2   John Garrett, "Learning from Ron Shaich," *Investment Masters Class* (blog), April 3, 2018, http://mastersinvest.com/newblog/2018/4/1/learning-from-ron-shaich#.

salivated over the small cap growth stock values in Hong Kong during the early- and mid-1990s.

Many listed companies met our prerequisite buying requirements in the depressed pre-Handover years, and these companies were frequently cash rich with almost no debt on the balance sheets. We viewed these caveats as a reasonable discipline to reducing risk in the volatile Hong Kong stock market. The added benefit would be the expanding multiple of all Hong Kong stocks we believed would occur after the Handover fears receded.

We strongly believed that, like Hong Kong itself, the Stock Exchange of Hong Kong would not only survive the colony's change in sovereignty, but also actually prosper. If Hong Kong were to flourish under Chinese rule, then the stock exchange, and the equities traded on it, would flourish as well. And the market was not insignificant by then, either. Hong Kong was the seventh largest market in the world—second largest in Asia.

After the collapse in 1994, Hong Kong's stock market began a slow rise to the run-up of the July 1997 Handover. China re-opened the Shenzhen and Shanghai stock markets in 1991. Mainland Chinese were given the opportunity of investing in stocks for the first time (Hong Kong was not open, though, to Chinese punters). In the summer of 1993, one million Shenzhen citizens queued to obtain stock application forms that offered a one-in-ten chance to buy stocks in Shenzhen companies. The incredible interest in this program overwhelmed the government application office where stock application forms temporarily ran out. The crowds became restless and started rioting, overturning vehicles and lighting fires. Military police arrived during the panic and restored order.

A similar happening occurred in 1996 in Shenzhen. Permits to buy listed "B" shares, which were originally created for "foreign" ownership only, saw ten thousand Chinese citizens again lineup at the government application window. The crowd became unruly and again the police were called in to keep order. The following day, trading volumes exploded to over HK$500 million in B-shares from HK$1million per day before the permits were released.

The Chinese had only one real option prior to stock investing and that was of depositing money into a savings account at the Bank of China. There were few alternative, suitable investment vehicles available to mainland investors since the communist revolution of 1949. The panic to buy, risking one's life savings, was something unimaginable to Western observers.

There was definitely huge interest for the Chinese in equity investing. This insatiable rush to buy headlong was, in some ways, a cultural thing. Available opportunities to profit were rare in China. If one saw an opening, he knew that he must rush through that doorway before it shut. I was always fascinated with this 'dismissing all the risk' thinking and began asking my Hong Kong Chinese friends and associates about the meaning. One answer, which I still ponder, explained that the Chinese believe you have a prearranged amount of fortune in your whole life, and opportunities arise that give you a chance to clinch your inherited gift.

I concluded, after witnessing the many instances where the Chinese chased their luck (and sometimes ended up like lemmings going over a cliff), that they must have felt destined regarding their entitled fortunes anyway. The losses incurred were, in their minds, not due to bad judgment. Rather, the timing wasn't right to receive their birthright fortune.

Cultural particularities like these run deep in Asia, and are not simply the result of political theory or governmental influence. The divisive state of Hong Kong ownership and organization does not easily alter such deep-seated cultural ways of thinking when it comes to the people of Hong Kong or Mainland China. I've always found it interesting that the richest man in Hong Kong, Li Ka-shing, fervently believes in the importance of Feng Shui. Among other things, Feng Shui is the exact measuring of a space, such as inside a home or office, to determine the wide variability of energies surrounding that space. Feng Shui, therefore, protects one by understanding which energies surrounding us are best left outside of one's own energy.

Li reputedly referred at all times to his Feng Shui expert and never made a move without first consulting him. On one occasion, Li tore down the famous Hilton Hotel in Central district and began building the sixty-one-story Cheung Kong Center—headquarters of Li's Cheung Kong Holdings—between the HSBC Hong Kong headquarters building and the Bank of China Tower headquarters. Even before the building was completed, Li was 'advised' to move into his new office, which also contained a private swimming pool and garden, on an exact date. I recall driving by the unfinished building in a taxi one night in late 1999 and seeing the top two floors curiously lit-up, the rest of the floors below were dark and abandoned.

Even a tremendously informed and immensely wealthy investor like Li never wanted to risk his luck. When it comes to the stock market in Hong Kong, it's imperative to understand the people and their ways of thinking, the means of production, and the deeper undercurrents of social and political change and direction. To be the best investors, especially as Western foreigners, we needed to gain a living understanding of the many aspects of Hong Kong and Chinese life, which meant seeing the companies firsthand and talking with people on both sides of the economic spectrum. Top of the list was getting to know more about the mind and method of the Hong Kong billionaire.

CHAPTER 7

COMPARING BILLIONAIRES

Li Ka-shing's success and acumen was impressive. Dad and I visited Li's headquarters in Central and were greeted by a tall, dapper-looking, and handsomely dressed Brit on our first visit. Cheung Kong Holdings was the main operating company of the wealthy Chinese Li family—one of the largest developers of residential, office, retail, industrial, and hotel properties in Hong Kong.

We were ushered into a dark-paneled conference room where the elderly tea lady customarily brought in the Chinese herb drink. Our host was courteous, allowing us gracious time to ask questions and be regaled with the many facets and personal stories of the company. It was a true rags-to-riches story; Li fled to Hong Kong during the Japanese occupation of China and became one of the most influential entrepreneurs in Asia. His company became one of the most successful companies in Hong Kong, a multi-national conglomerate helmed by one of Asia's most capable capital allocators.

As Americans, we easily established a distinct comparison in the gigantic investment genius between Li and Warren Buffett (The

Oracle of Omaha). Buffett's Berkshire Hathaway can be viewed as a portfolio of large public stock holdings and dozens of acquired private companies. Li's Cheung Kong Holdings were mostly centered on real estate development. Li's wealth was also generated from his holdings and investments in many other companies; including Hong Kong-listed ports and retail conglomerate, Hutchison Whampoa; holdings in Hong Kong Electric and Canada's Husky Oil. He had been an early investor in many technology/internet companies—including the online booking company Priceline (now Booking Holdings), Spotify, and Facebook.

Li Ka-shing, though, was not well known in the US. We became intrigued with the idea of possibly creating a meeting, an introduction, between the two billionaires. That Buffett and Li had never met became somewhat a mission for my father. As it happens, one of South Ocean's shareholders had a close association with the Oracle of Omaha, and Dad believed he had a friend through our host at Cheung Kong, he became excited about the possibility of introducing Buffett and Li.

Dad was more adamant in subsequent meetings with our Cheng Kong host, exclaiming he didn't want or expect anything in return for putting the meeting together, only that he believed Li a genius on the same level as Buffett—even though Li was not nearly as well-known for his investing prowess as was Buffett. Dad felt the world should know of the incredible talent and results of Li, and such a meeting would definitely be an interesting and enlightening introduction.

The share prices of the two billionaires' companies, though, diverged significantly since the Millennium. Hong Kong suffered quite extensively in the early 2000s with its volatile property market in a steep decline. After property prices peaked in 1997, real estate values began to decline almost continually until just after the SARS epidemic in mid-2003 (from top to bottom, residential property declined 75%). Cheung Kong's fortunes were severely affected in that downturn. The difference in the share values is reflected in the growth in the two companies' net book value (over the last ten years). Cheung Kong's book value has only grown 0.3% compounded annually whereas Berkshire's book value has increased 11.6%. That comparison is a stark difference.

My father's pains at arranging the meeting he wanted between the two supermen would have been an early introduction and recognition to the world of Li's accomplishments and shrewd judgment.

Our host, though, halted that idea and insisted it would never happen. I recalled him leaning forward and telling us of Li once flying to California for a meeting with a noted titan in US real estate. Li, evidently, got up abruptly from the meeting and left for the airport. When asked how the meeting went, our host said that Li responded, 'I don't do business with someone smarter than myself.'

Forbes Magazine estimates Li Ka-shing's fortune today at US$35.1 billion, Buffet at $90.8 billion. Li's fame has grown worldwide, not only from the Forbes List, but through his generous philanthropic and charitable efforts. Cheung Kong was a core holding in South Ocean's portfolios for many years, based on the remarkable capabilities of its founding chairman. Great managers are not found in abundance.

CHAPTER 8

SHIRTSLEEVES TO SHIRTSLEEVES

L i Ka-shing wasn't the only member of the wealthy elite I had the chance to observe and learn from while living in Hong Kong; another was a man named Alan. Alan gave me a broad smile when we met. He had a gleam in his eye, a happy countenance, and strength in his voice belying his advanced age. I felt an honored guest in his presence.

He was the father of a young man I met when invited to his yacht one evening by a broker friend. Alan was once titled "Richest Man in Asia" when he owned the tobacco concession for a Southeast Asian country in the '60s. I learned he became embroiled in the wrong side of a government coup and was thrown out of the country penniless. He then landed in Hong Kong and went on to make another fortune. You'd never suspect this self-effacing gentleman's immense wealth on first meeting him, though you would sense his authority.

Modern Hong Kong really began with immigrants fleeing communist China during the Chairman Mao and earlier Japanese occupation era. They began manufacturing cheap products sold to the West. Most arrived without a dime, leaving all their possessions behind. They worked 24/7 and amassed vast riches. This was the start of what Hong Kong has become today, one of the wealthiest per capita countries on earth.

I met numerous of these Chinese founders in the '90s. They all had the most modest and unassuming natures. Some garnered exclusive rights from Japanese brand manufacturers for Hong Kong, Macau, and China distribution. Others were hard-driving deal makers.

When I first arrived, I asked who was the English 'Tai Pan' (the title given a top foreign business person in Hong Kong/China) and nobody could identify one for me. The local Hong Kong Chinese were the real mandarins overtaking the long-established British trading companies. Long before my arrival, the British trading hongs, Swire and Jardines, were the most powerful Tai Pans.

Today, that first generation of immigrant Chinese founders in Hong Kong has mostly passed, with the sons and daughters—educated in the West—having taken over responsibilities for the family businesses.

As in most Asian cultures, the children who took over running the family businesses were overseen with stern instructions from the aging patriarchs. "Don't lose money" was the overriding catchphrase. I met one daughter of a shipping magnate, who lived in lush housing and was high in the social rankings of Hong Kong, whose only responsibility was rolling over a US$20 million portfolio of treasury bills.

Not long after our arrival, I was introduced to William. He was educated in the Midwest with a degree in the medical field but came back to take over the distribution business his father and mother started in the '60s. Like Alan, William's father was an unassuming man with a good nature. William was well-respected in the community and gave much time to charitable efforts, attending all the top social fund-raising functions in town.

The family's private company went public on the Hong Kong exchange in the early '90s, floating the minimum 25% shareholding to the public. Proceeds were to expand the then flourishing business into developing China. There was much promise in the outlook but the company stayed stagnant, overtaken by new technological innovations in its industry.

Twenty-five years later, the stock price is below the initial public offering price of the early '90s and the company still hoards most of the cash proceeds from the offering. William's sons, accustomed as they are to a life untarnished by hardships, are starting to be positioned into the company—he himself has pulled back from management responsibilities with most of his time spent buying properties around the world. Investment bankers, with eyes on all that hoard of cash, are whispering 'gold' into the ears of the sons over late-night karaoke sessions.

It's common for the founding 'fathers' not to believe in their children's abilities and talents. How can their son measure up to the past hardships they themselves had to overcome? Possibly to compensate, the parents send their children to higher educational institutions they never had the chance to experience. Higher education is of huge importance to the Chinese as it is the primary ticket to a better future.

Indeed, education just may be what keeps the wealth intact after the third generation that is now taking over Hong Kong's affluent families. But the mantra 'just don't lose any of my wealth' is a hard-paternal demand to overcome!

CHAPTER 9

JACK'S BOO-BOO

The following chapters describe my impressions on various excursions and trips across the border into China. The Middle Kingdom's rapid development and growth was astonishing in both scale and force. The sheer speed of its rise lay beyond the comprehension of most Westerners. I would have been largely skeptical of it as well if it weren't happening right before my eyes.

A preface, though, is helpful to understanding my expectations, interpretations, and the many misunderstandings I had at that time.

The late Jack Welch, former Chairman of General Electric, often visited China seeking ways of entering the massive, fast growing market. After two years of studying the market, Welch thought a high-tech light bulb factory would be a good investment. Soon thereafter, he found out that almost every local mayor in China was putting up a light bulb factory and there were more than 2,000 light bulb factories that had sprung up. This led to his admission of folly in a New Yorker interview: "I made a boo-boo."[3]

---

[3] Ken Auletta and Jack Welch, "Jack of His Trade," *New Yorker*, November 5, 2001, https://www.newyorker.com/magazine/2001/11/05/jack-of-his-trade.

Almost twenty years ago, Welch was prophetic in his statement about China's enormous growth and evolving competitive might. He entered the market envisioning the prosperous future of GE riding high in China throughout the next century. He commented that the biggest threat to governments was the giant competitive companies—an enormous force that would make past threats of Japanese dominance in the seventies look like a 'water pistol.'

In Welch's 2005 book, *Winning*, he made no less than forty-eight references to China and being competitive, mentioning at one point that it would take reducing costs by a third or more in order to compete in the China market.[4]

As Jack Welch presciently observed, getting to know China did not happen with short-term layovers in Beijing, Shanghai, or Hong Kong (though any first-time visitor would be impressed at the spectacular sights of each city). On my many trips inside China, I observed firsthand the complexity of Chinese culture. These visits inland revealed far more extensively the dynamics and characteristics of China's remarkable progress, evolving from basic agrarian existence to modern urban life. Any Westerner's brief trip, just witnessing the immense architectural and infrastructural achievements in China's major cities, would be superficial at best in regards to attaining a true perspective.

---

4   Jack Welch and Suzy Welch, *Winning* (New York, NY: HarperCollins, 2005), 342.

CHAPTER 10

INNER CHINA TRIPS

I made many visits into the heartlands of China which revealed the country's robust livelihood, bustling lifestyles, and the newfound optimism of the Chinese. One visit in 1994 was to Hainan Island in the south, just a couple hundred miles off the coast of Vietnam—a part of China which had not enjoyed any growth or improvement in decades. There I witnessed the massive infrastructural improvements just developing. We landed at a newly completed, vast and empty airport, which stood vacant in anticipation of the next twenty years of expected travelers (our flight was the only one arriving that day). The airport was built about twenty miles from the city outskirts, a fair distance from the beautiful beachfront resort area of Sanya. In 2018, twenty million travelers passed through the airport, a huge increase from the early days.

In Sanya, my friend Nick and I stayed at the south end of the half-mile-long beach in an old hotel in need of repairs. New developments planned for the beachfront were still on the drawing board and not yet evident. Our rooms overlooked the section of beach where scenes from the Hollywood film *The Meg* would be filmed decades later (a thriller starring Jason Statham and Chinese actress Li Bingbing). Sanya's development since then is unrecognizable from those early years when I visited.

One day I took a stroll along the water and passed below a shelterbelt of coconut trees lining the top of the beach. Crowds of Chinese lounged around in the jagged shade, fully dressed, holding umbrellas. On two occasions girls raced down the beach to snap my photo and then raced back under the trees; I must have been the first Westerner or 'Gweilo' (foreign devil) they had ever seen. At dusk, throngs of Chinese bathers descended from the safety of the shadows and splashed into the water. They wouldn't come down during the daytime for fear of getting a suntan (dark skin is a 'no-no' in Asian culture as it signals a lower rank of social status, like a migrant field worker).

Chongqing

On another trip in 2006, I visited the city of Chongqing in southwest China. Chongqing was the epicenter of heavy industry but thrives today from its rapid re-development. I enjoyed dinners in outside restaurants along the bank of the Yangtze River, eating fresh seafood under brightly lit skies of dazzling colored lights. Once a backwater, sleepy, run-down industrial city, it had transformed into a major manufacturing and transportation hub. Chongqing, with thirty million citizens, became the poster child for China's spectacular economic boom, posting double-digit growth for more than a decade. Though growth has slowed in recent years, the municipality is home to Changan Automobile Co., a state-owned automaker that has a rapidly growing fifty-fifty joint venture with Ford Motor Co. It's also home to Lifan Group, a privately-owned company founded by former political dissident Yin Mingshan in 1992 as a motorcycle repair shop with a staff of nine. Today, it is one of the largest motorcycle manufacturers in China. Listed on the Shanghai Stock Exchange with 10.9 billion RMB (US$1.6 billion) in sales, Lifan has auto and motorcycle production bases in Thailand, Iran, Turkey, and Vietnam.

In 2015 roughly 24.6 million motorcycles were sold in China compared to 500,700 motorcycles sold in the United States that same year. Due to laws prohibiting motorcycles now in China cities, China sold 'only' 16.5 million bikes in 2018. Chongqing hosts 133 motorcycle manufacturing companies and its automotive industry employs over 400,000 workers—a large percentage of the Chongqing workforce.

Further east stands the architectural marvel of the Three Gorges Dam on the Yangtze River. Quite an engineering feat, the eighteen million-kilowatt electric hydro-electric power plant supplied 5% of China's electricity (the annual power generation of eighty-five billion kilowatt hours is almost the annual electric power output of Argentina or ten big nuclear power plants).

The US had more than ten times the installed electricity generation per capita in 2006 than all of China. With still a lot of catching up to properly supply the future needs, four more such mega power plants were planned further up river.

The seventeen-year construction of the Three Gorges Dam was completed in 2012. It's six times longer than the Hoover Dam (at 1.4 miles across) and eight times more powerful. Ocean going ships move through the locks, allowing travel two hundred miles upstream to Chongqing—a twelve-hundred-mile journey from the ocean. It takes four hours for a ship to navigate through the six locks. The dam created an upsurge in commerce when China's interior opened after the completion date (think what the Erie Canal did for commerce in the USA). Twenty-seven million cubic meters of cement were used in the construction. That's enough concrete to make six two-lane highways across the entire US (Seattle to Miami). Unfortunately, a dead water zone has been caused by excess nitrogen, phosphorus and industrial wastes that have been washed into the Yangtze River. The migrating Chinese sturgeon, that once made their way from the ocean up past the Three River Gorge to lay eggs, have all but disappeared. In the last decade a program to release baby sturgeon just below the Dam has been inaugurated to replenish the giant fish.

Kunming

The city of Kunming, the high-altitude capital of Yunnan Province bordering the countries of Vietnam, Laos, and Myanmar, has a population of about four million. Many of its residents resemble the Thais, and evidently, Thailand was populated by the people of Yunnan centuries ago. Kunming built China's fourth largest airport. Much of the world's heroin is purportedly smuggled from the Golden Triangle into the Province and airfreighted from the giant airport. But the powerful illegal drug methamphetamine became a larger exported drug of China. Meth labs sprang up in many households in the lychee growing villages of neighboring Guangdong Province. There were so many labs in one village that three thousand Chinese police had to crack down on the illegal production during a sudden, large raid in 2014.

Kunming's many outdoor squares and parks are filled with large groups of older dancers singing and enjoying themselves to loud speakers day and night. They seemed to me much more relaxed and down to earth than their more business-oriented brethren on the coast. Electric motorbikes were everywhere, more plentiful than autos, due to the milder, year-round climate. The fabled mystical mountain utopia, Shangri-La, is a huge tourist draw. We weren't able to take a side trip there during our October 2012 trip because our group was to have an official visit to the steel mills where the city held a major commitment to producing the metal.

Kunming Iron and Steel Group is a State-Owned-Enterprise (SOE) with about thirty thousand employees. The major products are pig iron, bar, high-speed wire rod, rebar, hot rolling plate, and coking products. The managers of the SOE were hosting our visit to a newly built steel mill near the city. This mill produced less than ten thousand tons of steel, which was under the allowed production ceiling China had placed on its nation's new steel production facilities. China produces over 920 million tons of steel a year, followed by India at 107 million tons, Japan at 104 million, and the US at 87 million tons. Since the PRC had been actively addressing its steel production overcapacity, the Kunming SOE was evading the Central Government's rulings by building new but less efficient, smaller mills.

This circumvention was plainly evident as the adjacent land of the new mill we were visiting had a sign announcing the future building site for the next steel mill the SOE proposed. On our arrival, the welcome sign in the lobby naming our group's visit that day was evidence of the SOE's desire for our help in obtaining financing for the new expansion plans. More steel plants meant more needed employment for the city's workers.

The SOE and its industrial complexes are core to Kunming's economy.

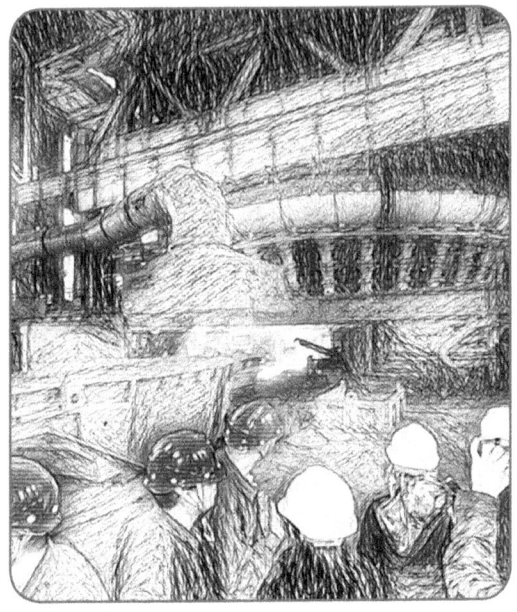

The other side trip I took was to a flower production facility owned by Hong Kong's Swire Group. The province has a large flower growing industry. Greenhouses are temperature controlled and house thousands of seedlings. At harvest, workers cut and wrap the roses in bundles, package them, and ship them to England where they sell for three to four dollars a bunch. Talk about low cost!

My inner China trips were insightful. As a foreigner, I view things with a different perspective. For one, all countries subsidize (China subsidizes steel manufacturing as the US subsidizes its farmers). But, do import tariffs answer the problem, making steel imported into the US from overseas the same price as domestic prices in the US? Protectionism leads to tit-for-tat price wars which are resoundingly detrimental for global economic growth. It ends up being a lose/lose situation for all countries concerned.

Realizing how countries function is important. It often crossed my mind on these trips that Western countries couldn't possibly compete with China's capacity to produce end products at dramatically lower cost. Striving to gain or win some dominance by producing higher-cost products at home is simply a losing proposition. China steel mills are not profit motivated, rather employment motivated. Mill plants are constructed on government lands, and wages are one-tenth those in the US according to the Bureau of Labor Statistics.

These advantages are vitally important to know when investing capital. To be best treated, it's imperative to know where the highest returns originate. Don't think you might sell your home-grown flowers to the local grocery, there are cheaper roses arriving in boatloads, cultivated from just outside Kunming city, heading for those same stores.

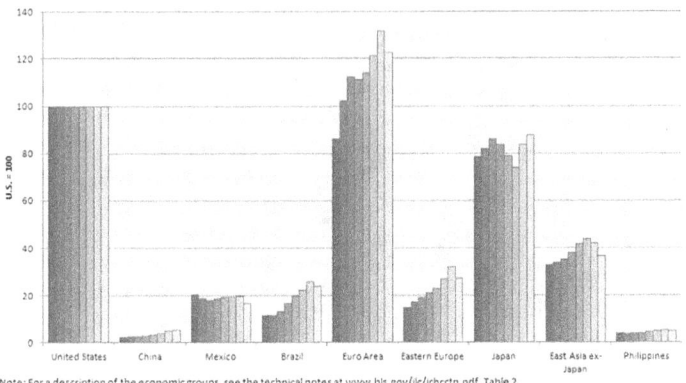

Average hourly compensation costs of manufacturing employees, selected economies and regions, 2002-2009

Note: For a description of the economic groups, see the technical notes at www.bls.gov/ilc/ichcctn.pdf, Table 2.
Source: U.S. Bureau of Labor Statistics, International Labor Comparisons.

Yangshuo

Near the southern city of Guilin in Guangxi Province, the beautiful village of Yangshuo has kept its quaint, almost western-styled boutique profile intact along the famed Li River. China keeps developing; sports centers and Sheraton Hotels are now being constructed in the largely terraced rice patty hillside areas.

On a boat tour of the Li River, we watched a unique fishing technique that was ages old. Trained cormorant birds—resembling a combination of a goose and a loon—are tethered by ropes to long, low bamboo boats. The fishermen nudge the birds over into the river to catch fish and then haul them back in to snatch the catch before they're swallowed. The picturesque limestone mountains rising above the area were the subjects of many famous Chinese painters.

Dalian

The seaside city located east of Beijing is where the tall, elegant Bo Xilai, who was once a rising star in the communist party, spoke fluent English to us at a conference we attended in the late '90s. Though he was later taken down in the corruption clampdown of the current administration, Bo Xilai was responsible for removing ten thousand choking smokestacks throughout the antiquated city limits, totally remodeling and modernizing the entire metropolitan area of six million citizens. Dalian is a model city in China. Quite an accomplishment.

There are many rural towns still untouched with China's urbanization and modernization. For instance, we drove to the grasslands of Inner Mongolia from Beijing. It was a ten-hour drive on rough roads. At one rest stop along the way, we were directed to some primitive concrete buildings way in the back lot of the gas station. These were the restrooms. There was no indoor running water or plumbing, just deep holes in the floors for your business. Entering the buildings, the wind was, luckily, at our backs and so the approach was not overwhelming.

Duolun

In September of 2005, we journeyed on a nine-and-a-half-hour drive from Beijing airport over rough, potholed-ridden roads to Duolun County, Inner Mongolia, to visit a start-up dairy farm. Chaoda Modern Agriculture, a Hong Kong-listed vegetable producer, had contracted with foreign cow producers to start breeding Holstein cows for China. China today has an increasing consumption of dairy products from almost nothing thirty years ago. Dairy cow population has been improving in China with the largest herds in Inner Mongolia. In 1949, there were only about a hundred thousand head of dairy cattle; by 1991, this number had increased to 2.945 million. Today, it's roughly twelve million.

In general, Chinese farmers are not highly skilled in managing dairy farms. Most cows are milked at a nearby milking station and the milk yield is only 10-15 kg/cow/day (roughly two to three gallons). In contrast, the average dairy cow produces more than seven gallons of milk per day in the US. A cow that is milking will eat about one hundred pounds each day of feed, which is a combination of hay, grain, silage, and proteins (such as soybean meal), plus vitamins and minerals. China's dairy farmers are learning quickly, though, as milk/dairy consumption is rising fast on the Mainland.

As an aside, one early 1990s visit with Philip Morris/Kraft Heinz management in Hong Kong revealed an interesting strategy of the well-known company on how it saw the China market. Because Chinese consumers were unaccustomed to milk, cheese and dairy products, Kraft Heinz's marketing strategy was clever. Once the Chinese got a liking for McDonald's cheeseburgers, which were rapidly expanding throughout China, Kraft would then start filling grocery shelves with their Kraft VELVEETA product lines. But only after they grew a taste for the 'foreign' delight.

In the northern grasslands of Inner Mongolia, it takes 20 mu (3.3 acres) to graze a cow. The thirty-year land lease cost amounted to 20 RMB/mu (US $3), paid up front. Chaoda estimated it would be able to sell excess grass harvests at 40 RMB/mu. The lands need further improvement, but at almost US$6/mu in grass sales (there are 6.1 mu to an acre), net production was estimated to fetch US$36 per acre. To compare, US grass production can yield substantially more—up to $52,000 per acre for organically grown cattle grass. Grass is extremely cheap in the underdeveloped hinterlands of northern China today.

Yet, when the railroads that we saw being built throughout the grasslands come into fruition, Inner Mongolian cheap grass could be shipped offshore to previously untapped markets. This brings to mind the opening of the Erie Canal in 1825, which was built to create a navigable water route from New York City and the Atlantic Ocean to the Great Lakes. When completed, it was the second longest canal in the world (after the Grand Canal in China) and significantly affected the development and economy of New York, New York City, and the United States. Cheap Midwest grains were exported through the canal and shipped across the Atlantic Ocean, bankrupting much of Europe's land aristocracy.

Grasslands in Inner Mongolia have turned to deserts due to the absence of any land management during the Mao reign. Consequently, to save the countryside, all the ranchers and peasant farmers were pulled off the lands and relocated. Local government brought in large new private farming/commercial enterprises, seeking to reverse the land from complete desertification. We surprisingly traveled past a test McDonald's potato farm on our visit that had just begun its planting operations. It was during this relocation and transition period in the '90s that Chaoda Modern Agriculture obtained this deal.

Desertification, from lack of land management, caused sand dunes to take-over the plains of Inner Mongolia. The author pictured keeping his balance sliding down one.

Towards the end of our day in Duolun, we were treated to an authentic Mongolian feast of lamb roast inside a yurt, where our hosts were dressed in traditional costume.

Returning to Beijing after our trip was like being on the road from hell. We stalled for seven hours in locked traffic jams, surrounded by overloaded trucks. All trucks to urban areas were allowed to travel only at night because the cities didn't want trucks delivering during the daytime, which jammed up the ever-worsening traffic crisis.

All those old, behemoth-sized trucks were equipped with lousy brakes and couldn't handle steep declines. They just edged slowly downhill. At various intervals down the mountains there were runaway ramps for trucks that lost their brakes, which was not uncommon judging by the number of tire tracks headed into the sand.

Ordos

On another visit to Inner Mongolia, we stayed overnight in the city of Ordos, a small district near the coal mining province of Shanxi. As we traveled by car into the city to stay at a new hotel, we were in wonder at the endless construction of newly erected, finished and unfinished apartment complexes, all with no inhabitants. It seemed as though it had been built and then deserted. These monumental residential and commercial edifices were developed under the assumption they would soon be filled with countryside citizens moving into the district. The city was undergoing immense building, with large skyscraper offices and residential towers unoccupied. We saw just a trickle of people walking around, and were scratching our heads at the scene. Ordos, with funding help from its rich coal miner neighbors, was expecting tourism and immigration on a rather disproportionately grand scale to arrive and occupy the housing.

While all this building was taking place, the area was often described as a "ghost city" by the Western media. CBS's "60 Minutes" broadcast a famous exposé on the overbuilt city in 2013. However, four years on, by 2017, the small overbuilt district had become more populated with a new resident population of 153,000. Forbes noted that "of the 40,000 apartments that had been built in the new district since 2004, only 500 are still on the market." 60 Minutes is scratching its head today.

Ordos has a history dating back 35,000 years. It is hugely rich in natural resources with 20% of the nation's coal reserves. Textiles (wool), coal mining, electricity generation, production of building materials, and bitcoin mining are pillars of its economy today.

Fuzhou Province

On a visit to the city of Fuzhou in Fujian Province in August of 2003, managers of organic vegetable grower Chaoda Modern Agriculture gave our small group a treat.

Our hosts drove us in vans over a magnificent tea-growing mountain range to visit one of the company's forty-one production bases. These bases were located in thirty different provinces throughout China.

On the vegetable plantation there were roads lined with deep irrigation ditches that separated the rows of crops grown under weather-resistant tents. This simple but carefully designed production process made Chaoda the most advanced private agricultural enterprise in the country. The company, with a total 23,000 acres under production throughout China, was further aligned with four top Chinese agricultural universities to cultivate and develop new, advanced varieties and strains of vegetables.

This particular production base, in Zhongming, was 225 acres of mushrooms, cherry tomatoes, beans, sweet corn and dozens of varieties of chilies, all grown under tight production schedules and conditions.

We spent several hours inspecting the growing methods and hearing explanations on why Chaoda-brand products are in such demand. China has forty-two million acres of vegetables under cultivation. Superior, organic growing methods, such as Chaoda's, were new to the mainland. Most of China's soil is contaminated from years of non-environmentally safe industrialization, thereby making consumers leery of heavy-metal food poisoning. Chaoda, with its sophisticated supply chain logistics management, transported its organic vegetables straight to markets, eliminating middle men and thereby allowing its products to be sold at market prices and commensurate higher profit margins.

A typical Chinese farm produces roughly twelve tons of vegetables per acre per year. Chaoda produced forty tons per acre annually from its superior growing methods and innovative techniques. Note how the pumpkins are grown off the ground in the photo of me and the general manager.

INSIGHTS OF AN AMERICAN INVESTMENT MANAGER IN HONG KONG

This was my first visit to the tea-growing mountain area of China. It is a remote region you won't find on any tourist map.

Almost as an afterthought, our hosts had a treat for us. They drove us to the nearby village of Zhongming. The village had a stream running through the middle where schools of 'lucky' carp are held in esteem and fed generously. Old wooden houses narrowly line the stream. The banks were fortified by villagers eight hundred years ago.

It was deemed a 'lucky' stream during the Ming Dynasty and a beautiful, rustic temple was built for all those seeking to have their wishes come true. We made a few new friends as we walked along the stream and fed the fish.

After a long day, we finished our stop-over with a glorious sunset before heading to dinner and then back over the mountain range for a four-hour drive to our hotel in Fuzhou.

My many travels into and throughout China were almost always long hard slogs, but all were most memorable. They helped me codify and understand the ways of this once isolated country.

CHAPTER 11

HONG KONG DISCONTENT

The relationship between Hong Kong and China is complicated. The crux of the affair centers on the two Opium Wars that took place off the shores of the city between Great Britain and China in the mid-nineteenth century, whereby Great Britain forced China to cede Hong Kong island after a naval battle resulting from China's seizure of roughly 2.9 million pounds of opium in nearby south China. Thus began the unique clash of political ideologies that has helped create the often-tumultuous history of their relationship.

During my time in Hong Kong, I've seen firsthand this spirit of excitement and discontent among the people. In 2014 I wrote about the Occupy Central movement, a civil disobedience campaign to dislodge the proposed reforms to the election requirements regarding Hong Kong's leader or Chief Executive. The reforms, demarcated by a White Paper written by Beijing, were viewed as a way for the Chinese Communist Party to pre-screen candidates. Students held mass sit-ins, using umbrellas to protect against the elements and police pepper spray. They slept in the streets, they made signs, they came out in hordes to demand the Chief Executive's resignation and to hold onto their liberties. Hong Kong has seen the evolution of the internet flatten and decimate its middleman role to the West since the turn of the century. Hong Kong factories, which long ago moved into China, have had margins and profits severely clipped over the decade leading up to 2014. Incomes barely increased over that time despite a booming economy. Over 50% of the SAR's population lives in brutal living quarters (a four-member family now has to spend nearly thirteen times their annual income to buy a four hundred square foot flat in an urban area) in this high-priced city-state. Unlike in the high-cost city of San Francisco, where newly graduated computer programmers earn US$100,000 starting salaries, Hong Kong graduates are not seeing a similar bright future.

As a society, the locals are normally non-confrontational. This is a conservative, parochial, fraternal culture that doesn't usually tolerate insubordination. Confucian values are at its core. A sign I walked by on the street really truck me, stating, "My parents are crying for me, I am crying for the future."

Today, five years later, Hong Kong is again in the throes of an even more contentious issue. In the summer of 2019, throngs of citizens took to the streets of Hong Kong and marched into major foreign consulates demanding leaders fully scrap a proposal that was unacceptable to Hong Kong residents. Chief Executive Carrie Lam set off mass protests with a plan to allow criminal fugitives wanted on the mainland and other territories to be extradited from Hong Kong and sent to them for trial. The concern here again is that the region's autonomy would be undermined by the legal system in China. After the late June protests, the bill was put on ice, but Lam's popularity plummeted. The Chief Executive said she would suspend the extradition bill indefinitely following protests that included two million people (out of a total Hong Kong population of 7.5 million). Though initially she stopped short of withdrawing it, under tremendous pressure, the CE soon announced the bill was 'dead.' The unresponsive reaction by the Hong Kong government and its snubbing of public opinion was badly judged and backfired.

In deliberating the relative values in the markets, we have remained invested in extremely cheap stocks listed in Hong Kong which have been under huge duress. One underpinning to our confidence is the Hong Kong dollar currency board, which 'pegs' the Hong Kong dollar to the US dollar. Coincidentally, this has been a major cause of Hong Kong's troubles as escalating property prices due to the peg have priced out many new buyers from owning a home. But as a buttress to financial stability, the Hong Kong Monetary Authority can defend the currency against most any devaluation scenario. China would also likely not want the instability of an improbable devaluation to hit Hong Kong. When China's capital account controls are opened and its currency becomes fully convertible, I suspect Hong Kong will link its currency to the motherland's RMB, but not before.

Our investments are not directly affected by the ongoing protests, but it is extremely distressing and sad for all of us who have lived in Hong Kong to witness the degenerating state of affairs. Hong Kong citizens are an extremely resilient, durable people that will see through its problems and excel again in the future.

CHAPTER 12

STOCK MARKET REFORMS

The following section relates to relatively recent events and developments of the Hong Kong and China stock markets. In early 2014, I made a case for a dramatic upsurge in global investor asset allocations to Hong Kong and China. I commented on the further reforms of opening China's financial markets to Hong Kong investors through the stock connect program or 'through train' as it was sometimes called.

> A recent proposal by the Chinese government to allow cross border trading between the Shanghai Stock exchange and Hong Kong stock exchange, linking the two exchanges, came as a surprise to the market last week.
>
> There was a knee-jerk reaction as wide price gaps between dual listed securities of the two markets narrowed.
>
> A similar plan was introduced in 2007 when Hong Kong investors were exhilarated with the prospect of a tie up with China. The Hang Seng Index vaulted, hitting all-time highs,

from an August 2007 low of 19,400 to 31,95 by October, as speculation gripped giddy investors of a 'through train' being implemented. China A-share prices rose to 60 times earnings, and Hong Kong's Hang Seng Index price earnings multiple was 24 times. Trading volume in Hong Kong reached HK$200 billion a day or US$26 billion (as compared to last month's average volumes of HK$6 billion).

Today, China shares trade at single digit P/Es and the Hang Seng at 10.3 times.

The 2007 ill-conceived 'through-train' plan was abandoned within four months. Share prices in Hong Kong and the Mainland collapsed and remain almost 40% below those peak levels nearly 7 years ago.

Thereafter, foreign ownership policies of domestic China shares, such as the QDII and QDFI schemes, were convoluted and ad hoc. Like the first B-shares (domestically-traded China stocks only available to foreign investors), created in the mid-1990s, these experimental campaigns were just testing grounds to the opening of China's financial markets.

Under the proposed 'through-train' scheme, there will be caps that investors will be able to make (transactions up to 550 billion yuan, or HK$691 billion, worth of Hong Kong and Shanghai stocks, net). This reform policy of lifting shareholder ownership restrictions is an important step to dismantling China's closed capital account.

The new reform is a significant step to the liberalizing and allowing the Chinese Yuan to become fully convertible. As China opens its financial markets to global investors, the impact will be significant. We call it the "Big Bang Theory." It goes like this:

Today's total world stock market capitalization is ~US$60 trillion.

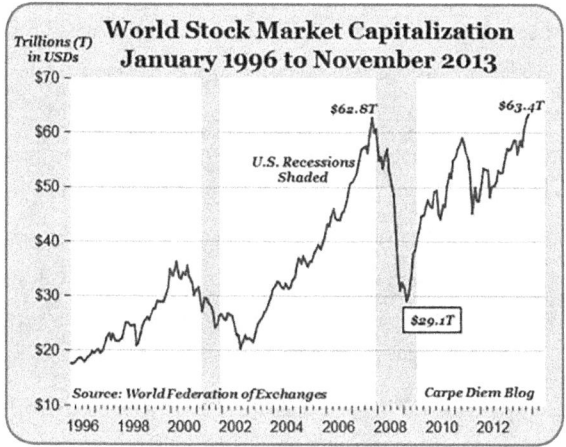

Hong Kong's stock market capitalization amounts to $3.1 trillion and is ranked fifth largest.

China's stock market has grown from zero, twenty years ago, to one of the largest stock markets in the world. The Shanghai and Shenzhen total stock market capitalizations together amount to US$4 trillion. China and Hong Kong combined amount to US$7.1 trillion. That compares to the world's second largest market, Japan, at US$4.1 trillion.

The stock markets in the China region are under-owned. Global pension assets, which amount to US$30 trillion, have only a fraction invested in the Greater China region. For instance, the relative weighting of global investment allocation to Japan was 12.5% in 2012 (down from 15% in 2002). For Hong Kong, it's was just 0.4%. And there isn't any allocation to China, yet.

To properly allocate weightings uniformly by stock market capitalizations, global asset allocators need to dramatically increase investments in the region. It will be years in the making. Bridgewater Associates founder Ray Dalio says 85% of US pensions will go bankrupt in the next 30 years, with $3 trillion in assets against $10 trillion in liabilities. He noted required pension returns are 9% and pension funds are lucky to get 4%. Moving these gigantic sums takes a lot of time, too, like turning a 747 around in a tight parking lot.

The new 'through-train' reform is a significant step forward. There are many regulatory issues and differences, of course, between the two markets that need to be ironed-out. Nevertheless, this should facilitate far larger allocations to the region in the future. When pension asset allocators are forced to increase weightings due to a 'combined' China/Hong Kong stock market, they will be unable to ignore investing in these stock markets anymore.

Presently, ICBC, China Construction Bank and Agriculture Bank of China shares are all quite cheap; they are also the world's three largest public companies (with Bank of China and PetroChina ranked #9 and #10).

With China's economic growth posed to overtake the size of the US economy, the cosmic shift in the global pension allocation universe is only just beginning.[5]

---

5   Brook McConnell, "The Case for Hong Kong: It is Different This Time. *Asset allocations to the region will rise and Hong Kong share prices are set to re-rate.*" April 14, 2014, http://www.south-ocean.com/monthly_updates.php.

I followed up this outlook again the following year with further thoughts about the cheapness of the Hong Kong stock market.

> As we have been highlighting since 2002—and more specifically in our April 2014 letter [see above], Hong Kong is a very underowned stock market. As we hypothesized a year ago, substantial capital inflows would be destined for Hong Kong and yet there had been little support to this viewpoint. Now, more and more banks and research firms are embracing this theme.
>
> One astute analyst (Louis Gave) stated last week Hong Kong/China was "The World's Most Crowded Trade." "… outside of a few Chinese retail investors, everyone is "short/massively underweight China:"
>
>> Today, China accounts for 15% of global GDP… yet, how many large pension funds, insurance companies, global equity investors, or endowments have 10% of their assets in China today? Or even 5%? We would venture not more than a handful; and this for an obvious reason: China remains an inconsequential part of most people's benchmark. But will this still be the case in a few years' time?
>
>> Goldman Sachs reported recently, "…active fund managers (are) still underexposed to the market, the rally isn't over…
>
>> But despite the rally making China shares more expensive, pressure for active funds to add more mainland exposure is likely to build… Funds of various mandates are underweight the market… (this) has

directly led to underperformance... and thus have marked benchmark stress and a need to raise exposure to China... If emerging market funds alone increase allocations in the largest underweight sectors in China to market weight, inflows could be worth $26 billion.

The opportunity set for active managers has been almost completely limited to the HK/China space, which may intensify the pressure for them to close underweight positions.

Goldman believes including mainland A-shares in the MSCI index would see significant, long-lasting capital flows into the mainland markets. (In 2019, global index compiler MSCI has quadrupled its weighting of Chinese stocks in its benchmark).

Credit Suisse expects further gains as the mainland liberalizes its capital account: "More legitimate capital outflow is likely to be the trend in China." (Our own contention is that outbound Chinese capital flows will be a recurring, key headline in the years to come.)

The meteoric rise in Chinese citizens' commitments in the mainland A-share market from the early '90s start of stock trading, dominating 80% of total transactions, still represents an underweight position in stocks in light of households' excess of savings. China is 'suffering' from a surplus of savings, with household deposits today standing at US$7.9 trillion (a 'high quality' problem. By 2019, savings have grown to over US$10 trillion). Nomura Bank (What's behind China's stellar market rally?) believes the real driver of Chinese equities is the direction of savings flows away from property and back into equities. One estimate counts mainland retail investor shareholdings in China to be worth RMB 13 trillion (US$ 2.1 trillion) versus wealth-management products at RMB15 trillion (US$2.4 trillion) and urban housing at RMB 150 trillion (US$24.1 trillion).

In our December 2013 letter, we postulated the potential of a much higher Hang Seng Index.

> With pessimism this intense and pervasive, we contemplate what the flip side might look like (should pessimism be replaced by optimism)? How about the Hang Seng Index (currently trading at ~23,000) rising to 38,000 in two years?

We presented this chart:

Fibonacci, the mathematician from the thirteenth century, constructed some basic numeric sequences. The above projection is generated from those sequences.

We reaffirm that outlook with the matching Hang Seng Index chart updated below:

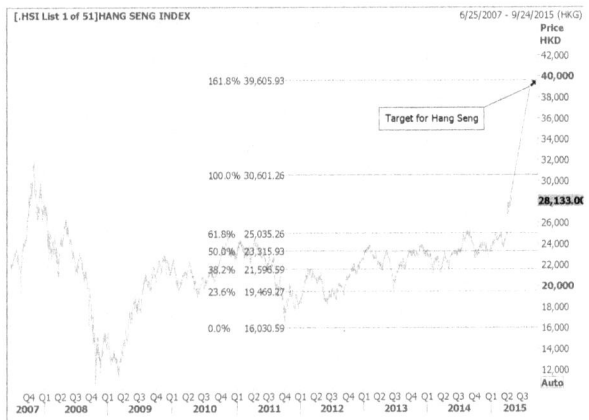

Laughable?

How is a 40,000 Hong Kong Index level achievable? A chart of the Hang Seng Index going back to 1980 overlapped with the monthly price-earnings ratio (right hand scale) follows;

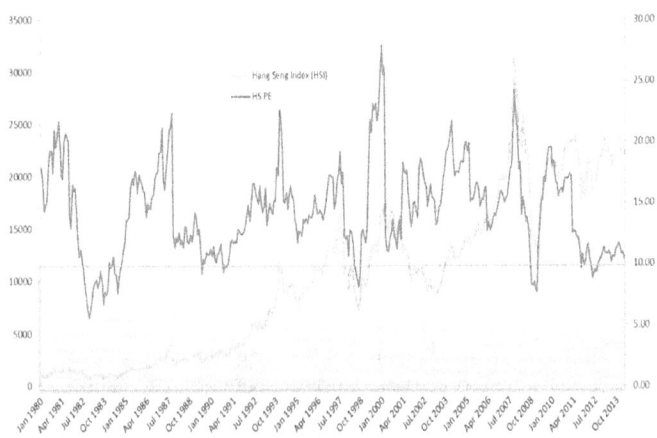

As history reveals, the main index has traded between a depressed P/E of 10 times and a high multiple of >20 times earnings. Consider this simple equation: with 2015 consensus earnings projections for the Hang Seng Index at 2,311, a 20x price-earnings multiple (which is below all-time historic highs) would equate to a ~46,000 level for the Hang Seng.

Additionally, China's FX reserves and its money supply are many times greater than Hong Kong. Stock prices in Hong Kong could see multiples far higher than in previous economic cycles purely on the facility to arbitrage differences between the two systems. It's not unlikely that our target of 39,600 could be markedly overshot; in 2007, mainland A-shares reached 60+ multiples!

The action last month is reminiscent of when I was a broker in Washington, DC in August 1982. The US markets made a bottom after years of underperformance and toxic sentiment. Depressed share prices bolted upwards when the bottom was reached.

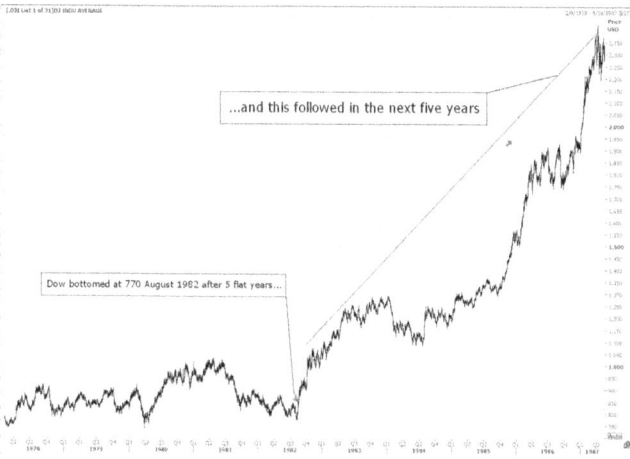

In the early 2000s, the China H-share Index followed a similar pattern. H-shares are those China companies incorporated in mainland China that are traded in Hong Kong. Their shares traded flat for five years, until mid-2003, then rallied from 3,000 to 19,000 by 2007.

The Dow Jones Average in the early '80s surged amidst much doubt (stagflation, Newsweek's 'Death of Equities') and began a twenty-year bull market. Like the 1982 market bottom, negative sentiment towards China's economy has been a dominant and prevalent refrain for years. At the end of the '82 bear market, reformist leaders had taken the helm (Reagan/Thatcher), as in Asia today (Xi/Abe).

The explosive 1982 Dow Jones rally came when no one expected it. Similarly, no one expects much from Hong Kong stocks today as the blue-chip index sells at 12 times trailing earnings and 9.9 times 2017 estimates, at the bottom end of its 30-year average PE range.[6]

In July 2015, though, Mainland China stocks dive 30% in a month despite government intervention to prop up the market (see circled in the chart below). By July 8, contagion from the mainland's stock market rout spreads to the Hong Kong Hang Seng Index, which drops 2,138.49 points—the biggest daily fall in history. Gains for the year on the index are wiped out.

The H-share Index has since that note made fits and starts. The recent trade wars stopped the advancing index, temporarily, yet the compression of China equity prices cannot be understated).

In late 2019, the China H-Share Index trading in Hong Kong sells at just eight times 2019 estimated earnings!

---

6   Brook McConnell, *April 2015 Client Letter*, http://www.south-ocean.com/monthly_updates.php.

As I write today, the US's trade war against China has thrown these fundamentals into doubt. Tariffs on imports and protectionism are never good for economies. Singapore's former prime minister and now Emeritus Senior Minister Goh Chok Tong said, "Overall, all countries will suffer collateral damage from trade protectionism and slower global economic growth." *When the trade wars end, as they will in time, cheap stock markets will rise.* The Hang Seng Index, as of February 2020, sold at a trailing price-to-earnings ratio of 10.9, closing at 26,129.93.

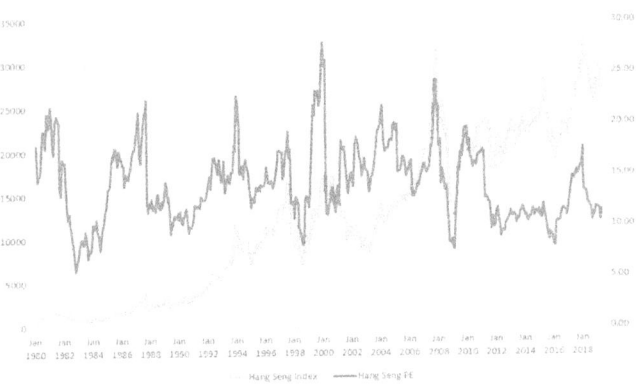

Updated thru July 2019: The Hang Seng blue chip index sells at the lower band of its historic price-to-earnings valuation.

The long-term trends remain intact and the next section delves into a few of the underlying themes demonstrating China's potential.

As investment giant Peter Lynch rightly noted, "You lose more waiting around for all the worries to be alleviated than investing in cheap, undervalued equities and markets."[7]

---

7   Tony Robbins, *Money: Master the Game*, 2016 Ed. (New York, NY: Simon & Schuster, 2016).

CHAPTER 13

CHINA IN TRANSFORMATION

Many accounts have been written about China, both pro and con, over the last several decades. Since the early 1990s, we had been closely following the topmost developments and dramatic progress of China from our perch in Hong Kong. All the while, the Middle Kingdom had continued to prove the many doubters and cynics wrong. It had not imploded nor collapsed, as best-selling books and short sellers contended. Though there have been many challenges, there have been plenty of positives as well, mostly unnoticed by the casual observer.

For instance, since the mid-1990s, with the onset of allowing private land ownership for China's citizens, real estate on the mainland has boomed. Today, new property developments witness frenzied scenes of Chinese buyers overwhelming application centers (like the first stock applications in the early '90s). Property speculation has become an insatiable pastime. The desire to invest their large hoards of savings in the real estate market quickened after the 2015 stock market crash in China had soured them on stock trading. Many

Chinese believe property ownership is the only avenue to attaining wealth. Property prices, consequently, have soared to levels beyond the reach of a majority of Chinese citizens. The government's attempts at dampening down home prices, with increasing restrictions on ownership, have been three years in the making, consequently slowing the overall economy.

Though the recent rise in home prices has outpaced income growth, there are many years of demand ahead for housing. China's urbanization, which is expected to continue past 2030, has led to its impressive economic growth. In the days of Chairman Mao, people were impoverished and lived simplistic lifestyles. It's taken three decades of economic reforms for China's population to move from being highly rural to living a modern, urban life. Another demand for home ownership is the key dynamic that over twenty million Chinese get married every year, on average. This single factor underscores a strong outlook for China housing.

As more farmers move from the countryside, cities will witness progressive economic development, requiring investment in infrastructure and urban services. New services and businesses will sprout. Education will flourish as individuals adapt to specialized urban careers versus simply sustaining themselves on the farm.

The scale of this transformation can be put into better context when compared to the US. America has three cities of three million or more inhabitants (New York, Los Angeles, and Chicago). After China's urbanization has matured, there will be the equivalent of a hundred Chicagos built on the mainland. The country is embarking on this build-out at present which means a lot of needed sidewalks, roads, bridges and rails are just coming off the drawing boards and into fruition.

CHAPTER 14

CHINA'S PROGRESS

China has steadily and strategically grown its economy, with an average growth rate of 9.52% between 1989 and 2019. While growth has retreated recently due to a cooling housing market and attempts to curb lending, China has evolved to become the second largest economy (using Gross Domestic Product or GDP)—yet is the largest economy in the world using PPP or Purchasing Power Parity GDP measurement. As defined by the World Population Review:

> PPP GDP is used to measure both the economic growth and living standards in a country. The PPP approach uses exchange rates to convert one country's currency into the other. Then, using a consistent amount of money, the quantity of goods and services that may be purchased in the countries are compared. For example, PPP may compare the cost of a car in France to the cost of a car in Japan (after using the exchange rate to convert yen to Euros, or vice versa) to

analyze the difference in GDP and cost of living between these nations.[8]

In other words, both economic productivity and living standards, using the PPP measurement, are now close to being on par with the top western economies. Reforms of its economy have catapulted one-fifth of the world's population from a once impoverished nation (not long ago) to a world powerhouse.

China has become the main engine of global growth yet is sometimes portrayed and analyzed in a narrow framework. At the start of the reform movement in 1978, China's GDP was US$150 billion and the US was $2.4 trillion. By 2007, the PRC was growing in excess of 14% and added roughly 5 trillion yuan (US$725 billion) to its nominal GDP. When growth slowed to 'only' 6.6% in 2018, its economy increased by US $1.4 billion (or double what it was eleven years earlier). The US came in with the second largest increase at $1.0 billion (according to the International Monetary Fund or IMF). To put that in perspective, China's growth for 2018 was 'only' the size of the entire economy of Spain or Australia (the thirteenth and fourteenth largest economies). Fully one-third of global growth is accounted for by China today.

This engine of growth has only started accelerating for China. Chinese household consumption has been growing steadily for years and last year accounted for 76% of its economy from less than 50% in 2013. China is the world's largest consumer market as its economy is no longer dependent strictly on trade. Based on IMF figures, the United States has the largest GDP in the world at $20.4 trillion. The second-largest GDP is China's at $14.1 trillion. The US has a

---

8 "GDP Ranked by Country 2020," World Population Review, http://worldpopulationreview.com/countries/countries-by-gdp/.

population of 327 million (the third highest population in the world behind India), while China's population is the highest at 1.42 billion. China's GDP per capita is US$10,000 versus $62,000 in the US.

Imagine, if every worker in China earned an extra US dollar more a day, or even just five dollars, where it would be in ten years, fifteen years, or twenty years? China still has a long way to catch up and reach standards of living enjoyed in Western economies.

The Chinese have recently been introduced to credit cards and mortgages whereby household debt to GDP in China has increased to 52% versus 76% in the United States. Household personal savings deposits, though, have also increased to US$12.3 trillion (January 2020) from US$2.5 trillion in 2007. The Chinese are savers, they value thrift and hard work, but there's still an imbalance in the allocation of households' financial assets, of which 42.9% were bank deposits, wealth management products (13.4%), equities (8.1%), funds (3.2%) and bonds (0.7%). US households have 55.7% of financial assets allocated to equities.

Though consumption spending is increasing, the average savings ratio of Chinese households exceeds that of American households by more than twofold.

There are 456 million households in China versus 132 million in the US. Total mortgages in China amount to US$3.6 trillion versus US$10.3 trillion in the US. Chinese buy homes mostly with cash versus debt. China's immense savings can be used to further facilitate the country's investment in domestic infrastructure and services as well as outgoing infrastructure projects, such as the Belt and Road Initiative. Transferring this vast source of savings to productive investments is key to the sustainability of future growth.

The long-term direction for China is to become self-sufficient. It's investing three times the amount the US invests in research and development and will become the world leader in artificial intelligence (AI) by 2030. Futurist Amy Webb, professor of strategic foresight at NYU, and author of *The Big Nine* commented, "Within a decade, all technologies—from everyday business to genomic editing—will in some way touch A.I. Today, China is poised to become its undisputed global leader, and that will affect every business." China, she said, is vastly "outspending, out researching, out-pacing and out-staffing" the US in future AI technologies in areas such as medical robotics surgery and drug discovery, environmental protection, public security surveillance, and data analysis.

Quantum computing, as explained by 13D Research, "… has the potential to be millions of times faster than even the most powerful supercomputers today. Quantum information operates on the physics of the subatomic world, making them capable of massive parallel processing." Often cited as being able to crack encrypted communications, the technology's disruptive breakthroughs in medicine, materials science, molecular biology, and financial applications are all being explored. China is the leader in research and development of this advancement.

The PRC cannot bank its future on US providers any longer and is relying on trusted (primarily Asian) suppliers. The intimidation by the US to cut off Huawei (a leading telecommunications equipment manufacturer that many regional US telco operators depend on) and other Chinese technology companies from utilizing US semiconductors will actually accelerate China's formation of its own semiconductor industry. China buys 60% of global semiconductors and is researching and developing advanced designs of tomorrow's semiconductor processors.

It seems only a matter of time before they'll be producing their own processors. And who knows what else?

CHAPTER 15

MADE IN CHINA

The Belt and Road Initiative is a global development strategy and is China's greatest international economic ambition. It involves infrastructure development and investments in 152 countries and international organizations covering a vast region from Asia to Europe, Africa, the Middle East, and the Americas. This region accounts for 64% of world population and 30% of world GDP.

Beijing's aim is to use this initiative to export China's technological and engineering standards, crucial to the country's industrial upgrading as well as strengthen its security interests.

In conjunction with the Belt and Road Initiative is "Made in China 2025."

Initiated by Premier Li Keqiang in 2015, this strategy aims to guide the country's industrial modernization, including the substitution of foreign technology with innovation developed on the mainland.

Li pronounced: "We will implement the 'Made in China 2025' strategy; seek innovation-driven development; apply smart technologies; strengthen foundations; pursue green development; and redouble our efforts to upgrade China from a manufacturer of quantity to one of quality."[9]

This strategy, known as the Chinese version of the Fourth Industrial Revolution, had initially raised concerns in the United States and European Union because of the mainland's goal to wean itself off importing a range of technologies from leading foreign suppliers.

The plan is to move China up the high-added-value manufacturing chain producing 'jetliners versus sneakers.' The sectors covered in the strategy encompass robotics, advances in hi-tech ocean-going ships, cybersecurity, nanomaterials, new energy vehicles and clean power equipment, advanced agricultural machinery, biomedical chemicals/drugs, and high-performance medical devices. China aims to establish dozens of national manufacturing innovation centers around the country to advance and develop its strategy.

The objective of 'Made in China' is to make the country more self-sufficient in an array of technologies and activities. The more productive/enhancing steps it can develop now, as its population ages (China's working-age population peaked in 2014), the better these headwinds can be mitigated and alleviated.

Another recent development is the Greater Bay Area scheme to link the southern Chinese cities of Hong Kong, Macau, Guangzhou, Shenzhen, Zhuhai, Foshan, Zhongshan, Dongguan, Huizhou, Jiangmen, and Zhaoqing into an integrated economic and business nucleus. The Chinese government expects the GDP of the Greater

---

9   Li Keqiang, *Report on the Work of the Government (2015)*, March 5, 2015, http://english.www.gov.cn/archive/publications/2015/03/05/content_281475066179954.htm.

Bay Area to reach US$4.62 trillion by 2030 or equal to Japan's entire economy in 2017.

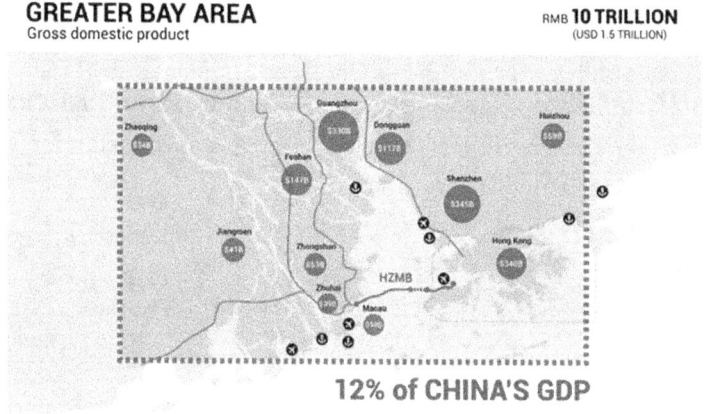

Graph from SCMP April 1, 2019

The South China Morning Post named several relevant aspects of the Bay Area:

1. The population of the Greater Bay Area is more than the whole of the UK and twice that of Canada.
2. The Greater Bay Area occupies less than 1 per cent of China's land area but contributes 12 per cent of GDP.
3. Air freight traffic across the Greater Bay Area is greater than the combined figures of the bay area of San Francisco, New York and Tokyo.
4. Three of the world's top 10 container ports are in the Greater Bay Area.
5. Macau, the world's entertainment hub, will partner with Zhuhai to boost tourism.

6. The provincial capital of southern China, Guangzhou, will become a transport hub.
7. Shenzhen's share of R&D investment is only matched by South Korea and Israel.[10]

With these developments as an overview, what will China look like in the next five to ten years? It's an important question for any investor to contemplate.

---

10   Eric Cheung, "Greater Bay Area: 10 facts to put it in perspective," *South China Morning Post*, April 1, 2019, Economy, https://www.scmp.com/native/economy/china-economy/topics/great-powerhouse/article/3002844/greater-bay-area-10-facts-put.

CHAPTER 16

THE CHINESE ARE INDUSTRIOUS AND ENTREPRENEURIAL

From a 3,000-year history of enduring cycles of prosperity and tumultuous chaos, China has a culture that accepts change. That inbred ethos allows for flexibility to rapidly adjust for future challenges. Dr. Shirley Ze Yu, a senior visiting fellow at the London School of Economics, fellow at Harvard Kennedy School, and a former Chinese national television (CCTV) news anchor, wrote in the South China Morning Post, August 8, 2019[11]:

> China's "996" work culture—working from 9am to 9pm, six days a week—is a blessing for the workers, as Chinese tycoon

---

11   Shirley Ze Yu, "Donald Trump's WTO move is a feeble answer to the China challenge," *South China Morning Post*, August 8, 2019, Opinion, https://www.scmp.com/comment/opinion/article/3021667/trumps-wto-move-feeble-answer-china-challenge.

Jack Ma of Alibaba noted, because many more people don't have the opportunity for work.

This comparatively extreme work ethic is partially derived from its recent debilitating existence under Chairman Mao Zedong.

Four years ago, President Xi started an anti-poverty campaign that lifted sixty-six million above the poverty line—they now earn 2,300 yuan a year or approximately US$340. Another ten million are expected to be lifted in 2019. There are plenty of extremely poor Chinese desperate for any work in China. Many Chinese, though, believe the main path out of poverty is through educating their offspring. They are willing to go deep into debt to help lift and alleviate their harsh circumstances. Education is of the utmost importance in the minds of most Chinese worldwide.

Dr. Yu continued:

> It is also true that China is both a rich country and a developing country. It depends on what one looks at: the status of the state, or the people.
>
> A single company in China has 500,000 couriers fighting for the opportunity to deliver food to homes on motorbikes, around the clock.
>
> Dashing between restaurants and homes, they earn on average 75 US cents each trip. On earnings that the developed world would despise, this willing labour force built Meituan Dianping, China's "Amazon for services", into a US$50 billion company.
>
> America's liberal market is unable to compete with state capitalism and its ability to mobilize state capacity. While China sets out to transform the Eurasian road map with

billions of dollars of infrastructure investment under its Belt and Road Initiative, Trump can barely get the border wall with Mexico funded.

If China's tech employees work 996, 'dispatch workers' have it worse.

The great unprinted story is how the Chinese middle class is investing their savings and starting businesses—an entrepreneurial explosion. Dr. Yu concluded:

> The US liberal market is also disadvantaged when competing with China's 18th century laissez-faire capitalism. It is entrepreneurialism at its most ruthless and primal, governed by minimal rules and regulations. In this system, neither intellectual property protection nor individual privacy protection trumps the instincts for entrepreneurial success.

In 2018 the South China Morning Post reported that Vice Premier Liu He, President Xi's top economic adviser, emphasized that private companies "were a crucial element in the Chinese economy, accounting for 50 percent of tax revenue, 60 percent of growth and 80 percent of urban employment."[12]

The private sector is being heralded as advancing China from a low-skilled manufacturing economy to a highly skilled, value-added industrial country. This shift from South China to the hinterland produces more balanced earnings and is bullish long-term for China.

---

12 Xie Yu, "China's private firms shy away from bank borrowing, delaying investment," *South China Morning Post*, December 20, 2018, Economy, https://www.scmp.com/economy/china-economy/article/2178954/chinas-private-firms-shy-away-bank-borrowing-delaying.

Many of the well-managed, private manufacturing companies we had been following, with major operations on the mainland, started diversifying out of the country many years ago. The PRC instituted mandatory 40-hour workweek rules and annual 20% mandatory wage increases for factory workers causing these manufactures to seek new factories in other Asian locations. The steady migration of lower-cost Chinese manufacturing to Southeast Asia over the last five years has begun to increase wages in Thailand and Vietnam to the extent where costs in certain sectors, such as appliances and household goods, can be 10% to 15% more than in China.

In fact, many manufacturing supply chains cannot operate outside of China's factory floor today. Plants with safety-focused certifications and capital-intensive machinery just aren't found elsewhere in Southeast Asia. Vietnam, often touted as an alternative, has less than 10% of the workers as in China. Moving out of China to other Southeast Asian countries won't happen overnight and a significant share of manufacturing will remain in China.

Beijing also aims to have foreign entrepreneurs work in China and is quietly cultivating its global recruitment campaign that started in mid-2018. According to the China AI Development Report (June 2018), there were 1,011 companies conducting AI or AI-related roles (20% of the world's total) and China had the second highest output of articles citing top papers on AI after the US.

The CEO of Huawei, the giant telecom equipment maker, recently claimed "about 50% of AI [Artificial Intelligence] scientists [worldwide] are Chinese[13]" and China is offering perks to entice

---

13 Ren Zhengfei, "Huawei Founder Ren Zhengfei's Interview with Chinese Media," interview by CCTV, https://www.huawei.com/au/press-events/news/au/2019/huawei-founder-ren-zhengfei-interview-with-chinese-media.

them home. Personal income tax rates would be cut to 15% in the Guangdong-Hong Kong-Macao Greater Bay Area for these highly skilled scientists. Shenzhen, the high-tech Chinese city bordering Hong Kong, announced it would begin a program to subsidize income taxes for technology workers who are most needed by local companies to live and work in the city. Taxes for qualified individuals would be cut from nearly 45% to 15% of individual income—close to the low tax rate enjoyed in Hong Kong.

With its innate entrepreneurial spirit in both the private and public sector, China will continue to nurture its widening potential, adding value to its own and the global economy. The PRC government is accommodating, and moves purposefully towards enriching the lives of its peoples and raising living standards. With their lives improving, Chinese citizens today are opportunistically and optimistically embracing the future.

Contrast that with many Western populations that are losing their trust in their country's governance, while Chinese levels of trust are swelling.

CHAPTER 17

REFORMS

From a totally state-run, centralized economy thirty years ago, dominated by large inefficient enterprises, China has reformed and opened up by allowing private, small and medium-sized (SMEs) companies to flourish. But several years ago, policies were introduced to help deleverage the explosive growth of the economy, with severe consequences for those that didn't adhere.

For instance, local bankers would be held responsible for any bad loans they made—for life. They couldn't be reinstated to their former positions until the loans were made good. For over two years, lending to the private sector was cut and smaller businesses were forced to obtain funds in the stock markets by pledging their stock. When margin calls hit, many entrepreneurs were rattled.

These policies are now being reversed and private companies are getting loans once again.

China is opening-up to the world and will continue to undertake a series of major economic reforms. President Xi recently committed to "deepened and sweeping reforms, (to) pursue quality development and expand opening-up." His speech was important as he outlined five significant reforms:

> First, we will expand market access for foreign investment in more areas. Fair competition boosts business performance and creates prosperity...We will work for the all-round opening-up of modern services, manufacturing and agriculture, and will allow the operation of foreign-controlled or wholly foreign-owned businesses in more sectors. We will plan new pilot free trade zones and explore at a faster pace the opening of a free trade port.
>
> Second, we will intensify efforts to enhance international cooperation in intellectual property protection. Without innovation, there will be no progress. Full intellectual property protection will not only ensure the lawful rights and interests of Chinese and foreign companies; it is also crucial to promoting China's innovation-driven and quality development. China will spare no effort to foster a business environment that respects the value of knowledge.
>
> Third, we will increase the import of goods and services on an even larger scale. China is both a global factory and a global market. With the world's largest and fastest growing middle-income population, China has a vast potential for increasing consumption.
>
> Fourth, we will more effectively engage in international macro-economic policy coordination. A globalized economy calls for global governance. China will strengthen macro policy coordination with other major economies to generate a positive spillover and jointly contribute to robust, sustainable, balanced and inclusive global growth. China will not resort

to the beggar-thy-neighbor practice of RMB devaluation. On the contrary, we will continue to improve the exchange rate regime, see that the market plays a decisive role in resource allocation and keep the RMB exchange rate basically stable at an adaptive and equilibrium level.

Fifth, we will work harder to ensure the implementation of opening-up related policies. We Chinese have a saying that honoring a promise carries the weight of gold. We are committed to implementing multilateral and bilateral economic and trade agreements reached with other countries.[14]

This remarkable speech on opening up China to the world has gone largely unnoticed by the US as the Administration continues to ratchet-up trade war tensions. The EU and other countries, as an unintended consequence, may be beneficiaries at the expense of the US.

---

14   Xi Jinping, "We will continue to advance along path of socialism, says Xi Jinping," *Business Standard*, May 4, 2019, excerpts from speech, https://www.business-standard.com/article/international/we-will-continue-to-advance-along-path-of-socialism-says-xi-jinping-119050400676_1.html

CHAPTER 18

FURTHER CHINA THEMES

In making the case for China and Hong Kong as underappreciated and emerging markets, we must also take into account numerous changes, happenings, and themes that are occurring at the ground level, and that are cultivating the region far beyond most of the world.

Government Reform

Two journalists from The Economist magazine, John Micklethwait and Adrian Wooldridge, wrote *The Fourth Revolution: The Global Race to Reinvent the State* in 2014. In the introduction, they describe the China Executive Leadership Academy in Pudong outside of Shanghai. The 'students' of the academy are China's future rulers, whereby the authors wrote: "The top jobs go to people of merit. The road to the summit is long and hard: You need to shine at… CELAP, prove your administrative mettle running a province (which might be the size of several European countries), and, increasingly, prove your business acumen by running a state-owned enterprise."[15]

Around ten thousand people a year attend courses at CELAP. Every Chinese civil servant is expected to have three months of training every five years—or 133 hours a year. Rather than some indoctrination school, it is more a symposium whereby "leveraging your skills, strengthening your global mind-set, and improving your presentation abilities" are emphasized.

Non-Chinese need to appreciate that reforms to China's society and economy will not include reforms to the central government. Domestic stability is the primary objective of the Communist Party after ages of foreign occupation, civil wars, and Cultural Revolution. The mainland Chinese, for the most part, are not unhappy with that arrangement as long as their livelihoods continue to improve.

China's government is trying hard to improve things.

Environment

On April 28, 2019, President Xi Jinping, attending the opening ceremony of the International Horticultural Exhibition 2019 Beijing (Beijing Expo), delivered an important speech titled "Working Together for a Green and Better Future for All." Xi said in his speech (as reported by XinhuaNet), "The development model of 'killing the hens for eggs' and 'draining the lake for fish' is at a dead end," referring to China's economic progress and industrialization harming

---

15 John Micklethwait and Adrian Wooldridge, *The Fourth Revolution: The Global Race to Reinvent the State* (New York: Penguin Books, 2014), 156.

the environment. "The future will be illuminated by eco-friendly development that is in accordance with the rules of nature."[16]

China began a decade ago to develop renewable energy and policies to improve its devastated environment from years of neglect. Today, China has hydro, wind, and solar farms in operation generating about as much renewable electricity as the rest of the world's combined renewable output.

Tariffs

The Trump Administration believes China pays the tariffs rather than US importers and consumers. Trump's fixation on the trade deficit with China is rather misleading. About 60% of China's exports to the United States are produced at factories owned by non-Chinese companies. Many multi-national companies have factories manufacturing in China for finished products to be exported back to their home countries.

"The U.S. business interests in China are much larger than what the trade data shows and the looming trade war puts these interests at risk," said a Deutsche Bank Research report from 2018.

Avon, GE, AT&T, Abercrombie & Fitch, Abbott Laboratories, Smucker's, Acer Electronics, and Boeing have all been in China for decades. These US companies either own factories or have contract factories producing their products. Some produce 100% of their

---

16 "Xi Focus: Xi leads green development as world's largest horticultural expo opens," XinhuaNet, April 29, 2019, http://www.xinhuanet.com/english/2019-04/29/c_138019499.htm.

products there, while others only produce parts or certain ingredients for their products.

Take, for example, the manufacturing heartland of recreational vehicles in Indiana, where US politicians like to stump about bringing jobs back to America. The industry sources most of the interior parts and structures all from China. US tariffs on steel and aluminum and other duties on scores of Chinese-made RV parts, from plumbing fixtures to electronic components to vinyl seat covers, are severely damaging that manufacturing sector.

General Motors is in China, but mainly to produce cars for the domestic market. I visited a new GM Buick plant near Shanghai. There were hardly any workers visible as assembly lines of cars were hung off the floor, on conveyors moving throughout the factory to different tooling stations. The factory was immaculate, all computer run, and it was so clean you could eat a meal off the floor. With the Chinese innovative commercialization programs, GM is able to produce localized model cars faster to market than from any of its other locations.

Protectionist trade wars are ultimately harmful to the world, but China's economy is driven by domestic consumption not exports. There is less dependence on export trade as net exports represented 1.1% of China's total GDP in 2018 versus 7.5% in 2008.

Millennials

With roughly 1.8 billion people born worldwide between 1981 and 1997, 90% of millennials now live in emerging markets. Continued domestic consumption will be driven by China's literate and digitally educated youth.

An article by AT Kearney entitled, "Where Are the Global Millennials?" described it this way:

> The Millennial generation—according to demographers at Pew Research Center, those born between roughly 1981 and 1997—accounts for 27 percent of the global population or about 2 billion people. Currently between 19 and 35 years of age, Millennials are in their young adulthood and, as such, are fast becoming the world's most important generational cohort for consumer spending growth, sourcing of employees, and overall economic prospects.

Millennials are expected to be the main growth drivers for demand of ecommerce and digital services, where buildout of 5G infrastructure and services will certainly augment those drivers. They make 75% of all online transactions today, according to PWC.

Chinese millennials alone (351 million) outnumber the entire population of the US. That age group is an important source of consumer spending, and will be a spearhead of balanced economic growth for China in the coming years.

CHAPTER 19

INVESTORS NEED TO TURN AWAY FROM THE CROWDED US TRADE

The rules that govern a public company listed in China's stock exchanges are different than for companies listed on the Hong Kong Stock Exchange. Both of these exchanges have similar listing requirements that you would see in US stock exchanges whereby companies have to report timely financial statements, produce audited results, and meet other requirements of size and capitalization, the difference is in the accounting rules which differ in China and are unlike generally accepted accounting principles (GAAP) used in Hong Kong and the US. China is still an immature stock market—bank capital, rather than equity capital, is still the main source of providing funds for commercial growth.

Yet, the greater Chinese stock markets of Hong Kong and China are just starting to gestate. There's little optimism in the markets today and that entirely misses the huge opportunity in the coming years.

Take the assumptions of growth and indebtedness of East versus West. By 2020, the US federal budget net interest bill will be more than $150 billion higher than in 2018, but the economic growth at 2% will unlikely be able to service the debt. On the other hand, emerging markets are likely to grow 4.7% in 2019, almost double the US figure (and China's growth will likely be even higher).

Projected economic growth of less-developed markets is higher but they also enjoy lower levels of gross public indebtedness relative to GDP. Asian countries have a higher proportion of fixed-investment driving GDP growth and consumption. Fixed investment in infrastructure are 'roads' built for the future. China now has the largest highway system in the world, enough to go around the globe more than three times. Former Chinese Prime Minister Zhu Rongji once commented, 'I don't mind borrowing a dollar today to get back three in three to five years.'

At the end of 2018, total government debt stood at about US$ 5.2 trillion and Chinese local governments may have an additional $5.8 trillion in off-balance sheet debt. That amounts to just about 100% of GDP. This high debt level, as seen by investors, is a current economic concern facing China.

In the US, the national debt reached a new milestone earlier this year topping $22 trillion for the first time, or about 100% of GDP. Forty percent of this debt is held by foreigners. The US government's unfunded liabilities (social security, etc.), though, are an additional $46 trillion, and total US unfunded pension obligations may be as high as $200 trillion (talk about off-balance sheet debt)!

China's gross debt is often double counted. State-Owned Banks lend to State-Owned Enterprises. As one analyst put it, 'in a way, the Communist Party is lending to the Communist party.' And, importantly, most of the loans are domestic obligations with little foreign debt owed to non-Chinese lenders. In fact, one of the main causes of the severity of the 1997 Asian Financial Crisis was that countries which owed a lot to foreign lenders (especially Japanese banks) had the loans yanked as the crisis mounted, thereby deepening the overall economic decline.

China is not obligated to outsiders.

Together with its rapidly expanding middle class and cheaper equity valuations, China-oriented investors are offered a compelling risk/reward opportunity today.

Historically, the biggest stock market returns have come with the fastest growing economies. But that pattern changed in recent years as investors chased technology and the pursuit of growth at any cost—at the expense of everything else. Many stocks in Hong Kong and China today languish at extremely attractive levels.

Morgan Stanley Investment Management chief global strategist, Ruchir Sharma, wrote an article in 2018 about the opportunities that lie in the overlooked corners of the globe—the places where prices have stagnated at depressed levels for years and yet economic growth has exceeded that of the Western world.[17]

Another recent article from Fortune Magazine journalist Shawn Tully argued that with the MSCI EAFE Index (emerging market index) trading near a fifty-year low relative to the US market, now is a

---

17 Ruchir Sharma, "When the Bubble Bursts, Consider the Anti-Bubble," *New York Times*, December 29, 2018, Opinion, https://www.nytimes.com/2018/12/29/opinion/tech-bubble-bursting-stock-market.html?auth=linked-google.

good time to reallocate to under-invested, less-crowded markets of the global economy. He closed the article, "When pessimism is much too high, and prices are much too low, that's the perfect time to pounce."[18]

Towards the end of 2018, the *Financial Times* reflected on why Asia was likely to outgrow the rest of the world: "In the next seven years, another 1bn people are expected to join the emerging middle class, according to the Brookings Institution. Of this, about 90 per cent are likely to be Asian, of which about 500m will be Indian and 300m Chinese."[19]

Asia is growing and the West is bloated. Asia's indebtedness is lower and the East does not have the ever-growing entitlement spending (with interest expense on mounting debt levels and social spending on aging baby boomers) that inhales an ever-larger share of the US budget. The longer-term outlook favors the faster growth nations residing in Asia ex-Japan economies.

---

18 Shawn Tully, "Why Emerging Markets are a Screaming Buy," *Fortune*, November 20, 2018, https://fortune.com/longform/best-investments-2019-emerging-markets/
19 Christian Déséglise, "Sell-off shunts some emerging markets into bargain territory," *Financial Times*, Dec 2, 2018, Opinion, https://www.ft.com/content/bba3fc26-dc39-11e8-b173-ebef6ab1374a.

CHAPTER 20

CHINA: A CURRENCY MANIPULATOR

Over 150 countries do the majority of their trade with the Middle Kingdom, and only 19% of China's exports go to the US. As China's economic growth has slowed and the US exchange rate has recently risen against most currencies, the US administration has cited China as a currency manipulator.

About 80% of China's trade is with countries other than the United States. A nation does not lower its currency to impact 20% of its trade at the expense of the rest of its trading partners. The yuan exchange rate is set daily by the People's Bank of China (PBOC) to a basket of major world currencies and aligns it to those currency movements. The recent yuan exchange rate lowered to a 7:1 ratio with the US dollar, which is not out of line with the advancement of the USD and is in line with market forces and global trends. The recent hysteria of a weakening yuan is likely overblown.

It is not in China's interest to have a lower value on its currency. The major property developers in China, for instance, have tons of US dollar denominated debt that becomes more difficult to pay with a lower RMB. Lowering the currency also imports inflation.

To define a nation as a currency manipulator—a designation applied by US government authorities—there are conditions that must be met. Economists generally say it occurs when a country that runs a large overall trade surplus buys foreign currency, often dollars, to keep its currency from rising in value, because that weaker currency gives its exporters an edge. China doesn't currently have a large current account surplus and hasn't been buying foreign exchange to lower its RMB rate. With foreign exchange reserves at a stable level of around US$3.1 trillion (the world's largest), China actually sold foreign exchange last year and hasn't been buying nor selling large sums in 2019.

Currencies today float and actively change in value. Fixed exchange rates went out with the end of the Bretton Woods system in 1971. Examine the trend of the dollar against other major world currencies and you will discover the same trend of the dollar against the yuan. Politicians simply follow the pre-Bretton Woods, academic view of currencies when they pronounce China a currency manipulator.

• • •

Since early 1995, I've been observing the continued progress of China in my monthly client reports from Hong Kong. It is amazing today how much misinformation, distortion, and poor analysis is rehashed constantly about the status and future direction of China. It seems the West has suddenly woken to the competitive threat it faces and is hitting back. China is the whipping boy for Western societies' shortcomings and it is probably as bad now as it has ever been.

To highlight this, there's a passage in Andrew Carnegie's autobiography that hits home. Carnegie, a penniless Scot who immigrated to the US with his parents in 1848 and became the richest man in the world, was discussing with William Gladstone the inconceivable notion that America, at the time, was so little referenced in Europe.

The British Prime Minister asked Carnegie about the population of the United States:

> "Sixty-six millions, and yours is not much more than half."
>
> "Ah!, yes, surprising!"
>
> With regard to the wealth of the nations, it was equally surprising for him to learn that the census of 1880 proved the hundred-year-old Republic [America] could purchase Great Britain and Ireland and all their realized capital and investments and then pay off Britain's debt, and yet not exhaust her fortune… I pointed out that America was now the greatest manufacturing nation in the world… British manufactures in 1880, eight hundred and sixteen millions sterling; American manufactures eleven hundred and twenty-six millions sterling. His one word was:
>
> "Incredible!"
>
> [Gladstone then asked,] "Why does not some writer take up this subject and present the facts in a simple and direct form to the world?"[20]

---

20   Andrew Carnegie, *Autobiography of Andrew Carnegie*. (Boston; New York: Houghton Mifflin Company, 1920).

It is unfortunate that many in the West only view China from its imperfections and deficiencies of the past. China is still only in its early developmental stage, as America was in 1882, and there will be, undoubtedly, many more stumbles in its future. Yet, the PRC addresses these inadequacies and takes remedial actions to correct. Indeed, China was closed to the outside world for a time but it has developed far more than is commonly known. Deng Xiaoping's famous saying, "crossing the river by feeling the stones," aptly describes the process China applies in its pioneering efforts of opening to the world.

CHAPTER 21

THE BANQUET SYSTEM

One challenge I labored at since our founding was in developing a viable systematic approach to owning stocks. Dad began his second Wall Street career after the 1974 crash where he and his partner utilized an out-of-favor screen. By employing the Value Line top capitalized stock universe, their system was to order stocks in decile rankings of 1 to 10, whereby the top 1 decile group were stocks selling at their lowest historic ten-year multiple to projected twelve-month earnings. The Decile 1 ranking usually identified stocks of companies that had lost their stockholder support or backing but not their potential earnings power.

Dad's systematic approach was what I tried to implement for our investment method when we arrived in the early '90s only to find it didn't apply. In 1992, the Hong Kong stock market was less than US$200 billion in total market size. Though the early '90s saw many smaller companies being listed, the larger cap stocks were valued mainly as asset plays versus earnings growth stocks. Most of the biggest stocks were property developers or banks with little historic ratios to base a system like Dad's. Property projects were completed in lumps, over years of development, and generally were not reporting quarter over quarter growth of earnings.

We began using a basic approach that would look to own smaller/middle sized growth companies where the price-earnings multiple was half of the expected growth rate, or the Price/Earnings to Growth ratio (PEG).

After years of analyzing and testing many investment systems, I wanted a screen that was simple to understand but would capture all the investment system approaches as well. Then a colleague of mine in Hong Kong named Bob Howe sent me a manual in early 2011 entitled *The Buffett Way* by Darrin Donnelly. Buffett is well known as a long-term investor who buys great companies when they are available at reasonable prices. After reading this guide book, I immediately sensed it was quite viable in comprehensively screening Hong Kong's 1,600 stock listings. With the assistance of some very bright software developers at Reuters, I began developing our in-house software program for owning equities, analogous to Warren Buffett's approach.

The strategy is a discipline based on long-term value investing—we invest in businesses versus merely a stock's price. We believe that short term fluctuations in stock prices are generally meaningless with this 'business owner' mentality, as stock prices eventually reflect the true value of a business. We are able to examine and analyze any stock to buy, hold, or sell instantly using this system.

After more than a year of development and testing, we launched our system in 2011 for investing our clients' monies in the Hong Kong stock market. The system identifies or screens for mispriced, out-of-favor stocks to own. Our portfolios are made up of leading Hong Kong-listed enterprises that are doing business in the fastest growing large economy on earth—China.

We named our screen the "Banquet System." The program is not a computer-run, black box, nor is it a quantitative tool, but rather a diagnostic tool that unearths and discovers quality companies selling at reasonable prices.

The system operates along two analytical premises.

The first is the analysis of the quality of a business. The system renders a rating based on five fundamental inputs. Any company with a return-on-equity (ROE) of 12-15% receives a 1-point rating (a ROE of 15-20%, a 2-point rating, 20-30%, a 3 rating and above 30% ROE scores a full 4 points). Second, if a company's net income has grown every year for past five years, it gets the highest rating of 4 points. If one year was down in the five years, the company gets 3 points. The same point scoring measure is used with the next fundamental input, cashflow (from operations) over the past five years. The fourth input is a scoring on profit margins, where the current profit margin is compared to the average profit margin of the company over the past five years and its latest profit margin is compared to peers, with the highest score being 2 points. The last fundamental input scores 2 points if net income of the company can pay off all long-term debt within six years, 1 point for over six to fifteen years, and zero points if repayment of long-term debt takes longer.

The highest rating score is 17 points, or an A rating. Scores of 7 to 12 rate B, lower than 7 points is a C rating. With this rating system, we can uncover stocks of fundamentally sound businesses to own and, when purchased at reasonable prices, they tend to out-perform over a longer-term horizon.

The second premise estimates an intrinsic value. This value is what we might expect to sell the entire business for in five to ten years. We aim to buy at a reasonable price today to hold for our target price to sell in the future.

To calculate intrinsic value, a ten-year target price is calculated. The ten-year target price is the ten-year forward estimated earnings per share figure times the lowest, annual five-year price-earnings multiple. This ten-year earnings per share figure is calculated by compounding trailing twelve-month earnings per share (EPS) using Reuters' StarMine estimated growth rates. (A StarMine discounted growth rate is more judicious than the consensus, market growth rate estimates because analysts generally tend to be slightly over-optimistic with their projections.)

The ten-year future EPS figure is multiplied by the lowest annual P/E over the past five years to calculate the future target value, which is then discounted to a maximum price we would pay today for our required 15% annual return (a return that is more than double the market return).

To avoid being overly optimistic, our controls use very reasonable growth of earnings estimates and the lowest annual price earnings multiple to calculate intrinsic value. This adds to our margin of safety.

We screen all Hong Kong stocks and focus our fundamental analysis on those top-rated stocks selling at or below our maximum purchase price. We endeavor to meet management of each company to better understand the company's fundamentals and outlook. We further analyze the competitive advantages of a company, questioning whether the company will be around for the next ten years, or will competition/technology or some other disruptive occurrence eat away at profits.

Our Banquet System helps to identify and recognize cheap, out-of-favor values where we seek to own small/mid-capitalized shares of fast-growing, Hong Kong-listed companies with businesses that are benefiting from operations in China.

Out of favor stocks don't always outperform every year. In 2017, for instance, the Hang Seng Index gained 35% whereby 20 points of the 35-basis point gain was accounted for by the outperformance of just one stock that year. That 'darling' technology stock, which gained >100% and traded at a very high multiple to earnings (close to a hundred times at the high), subsequently fell by as much as 38% in the following year (2018). Cyclical and speculative real estate stocks rose in 2017, sectors we also avoided.

Side-stepping huge losses by avoiding and not getting seduced by the in-favor sectors is a key factor to mitigating risk using our Banquet System approach. Though we may raise cash levels in our concentrated portfolios when we can find few stock opportunities to invest, our positioning in cheap, out of favor stocks tends to outperform over longer cycles.

CHAPTER 22

THE LYNCH MODEL

In the third quarter of 2018, we further enhanced our in-house stock selection process with an overlay developed by Peter Lynch of Magellan Fund. This evaluation approach aligns well with our intrinsic value screen, the Banquet System, with some additional elements.

In his method of analysis, Lynch charted the stock price and the earnings per share together and aligned the value of $1 in earnings per share to $15 in stock price. He wrote in his book *One Up on Wall Street*:

> A quick way to tell if a stock is overpriced is to compare the price line to the earnings line. If you bought familiar growth companies when the stock price fell well below the earnings line, and sold them when the stock price rose dramatically above it, the chances are you'd do pretty well.[21]

---

21 Peter Lynch and John Rothchild, *One Up on Wall Street*, 2nd ed. (New York: Simon & Schuster, 2000), 164-65.

Lynch defaulted his earnings line multiple to fifteen times for all growth stocks. The tweak for our screen is to be flexible with the multiple. We can use an individual stock's lowest annual price-earnings multiple over the last five years, (similar to our Banquet System process), and we can draw the earnings line using any meaningful multiple assumed, as well.

For example, one current holding of ours is Beijing Enterprises Water Group Ltd (BEWG, code 371hk), which had normally sold at almost twenty times its earnings annually over the past six years. The lowest the shares sold relative to its annual earnings was fifteen times.

In late 2018, the share price of BEWG was selling below the earnings line (light gray), which signals the risk/reward of owning this growth stock as attractive.

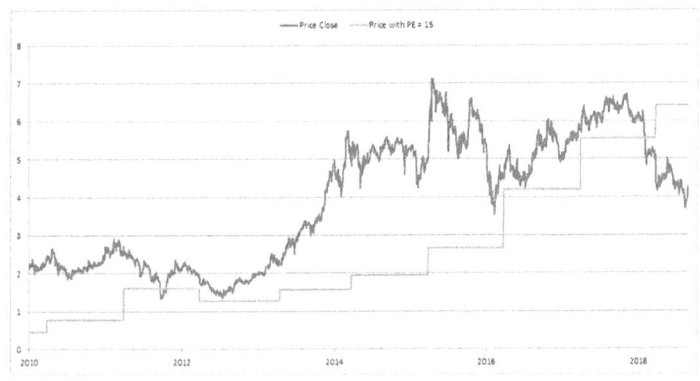

BEWG is also attractive and rated a buy on our intrinsic value Banquet System screen. As shown by the dark line, the share price today is selling below the earnings line.

We added to this longtime holding after the company announced above average earnings growth in its August 2018 financial report.

The next is an example of an initial purchase in the 3rd quarter of 2018 of BYD Electronic (code 0285hk), a leading manufacturer of smart phone casings. The ranking on our Banquet System intrinsic screen of the company's fundamentals was favorable and the company had enjoyed consistent earnings growth over the past consecutive four years. The balance sheet had net cash with no long-term debt. The share price had fallen from a 52-week high of HK$25 to HK$8 where we began buying:

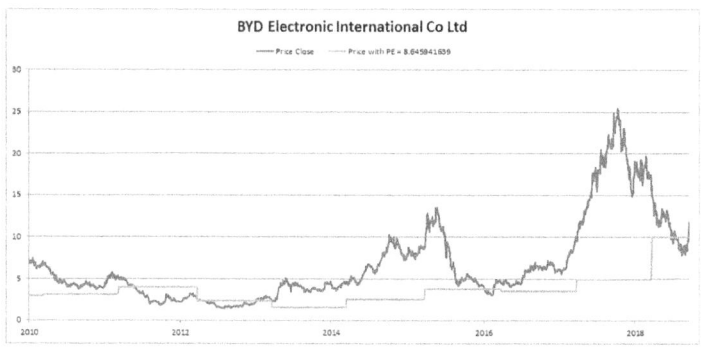

Another example in 2018, we purchased A-rated toll road and bridge operator Jiangsu Expressway Co. (code 0177hk). The Nanjing-based company, in the busy Yangtze River delta area, had seen steadily rising earnings from increased toll revenues and was expanding its portfolio of toll roads and bridges in the Jiangsu Province. The company paid a generous 5.4% dividend. With an expected 6% long term growth rate, the shares were attractively priced based on our Banquet System screen.

We began buying when the share price dipped below the light gray earnings line (earnings per share times lowest annual five-year price earnings ratio).

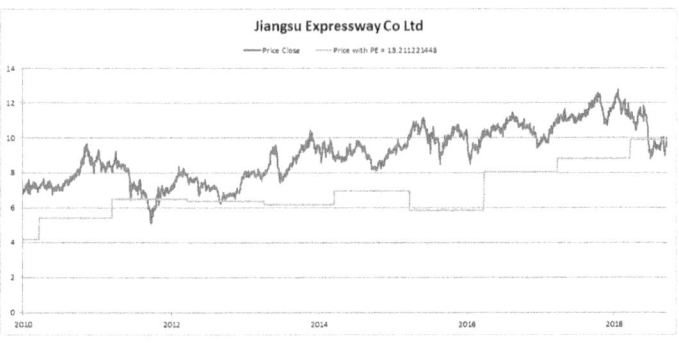

Back then, we also added to our position in A-rated China State Construction (code 3311hk) on weakness when the price was close to $7.40/share.

These examples show how we apply our discipline of buying quality growth companies that have lost their favor in the market, yet offer better risk-adjusted returns. Our combined processes (Banquet System/Lynch System) pinpoint more accurately the risk/reward, overpriced/under-valued areas of the market. As we continued fine-tuning and upgrading our internal processes, we became better able to identify and delineate many more opportunities in the less-followed small/mid cap stock sectors in Hong Kong.

This system works well for investing in the Hong Kong stock market. After the sharp stock market correction in July 2015, for instance, quality company share prices rebounded and 'survived' versus the lower quality, speculative stocks that had risen spectacularly during the earlier bull rally in the year.

We have often waited through extended periods in Hong Kong when investors lacked interest and our holdings slumped. Yet when our systems have indicated the cheapness of a particular holding, we would not deviate from our discipline by selling an undervalued stock just because it wasn't performing well. On many occasions, when we have held while these dull-performing and misunderstood stocks lagged, we would frequently be rewarded. Insiders and company management that know well the value of the company, will strategically act on the low valuation in the market and announce they'll take the company private at a much higher price premium. Of course, these catalysts come out of the blue and generally can't be anticipated, but this does substantiate our systems' quantitative soundness. Just because a stock is out of favor and not the current market 'flavor of the month' does not necessarily invalidate its attractiveness.

Further confirmation on investing in quality small/mid cap stocks was outlined in a study entitled "Size matters, if you control your junk."[22] The study demonstrated that, when all other things are equal, the stocks of "quality" smaller companies have beaten the market by a country mile.

Owning strong smaller company stocks at reasonable prices is a recipe for great returns.

---

22 Asness, Clifford, Andrea Frazzini, Ronen Israel, Tobias J. Moskowitz, and Lasse H. Pedersen. "Size matters, if you control your junk." *Journal of Financial Economics* 129, no.3 (2018): 479-509.

CHAPTER 23

FINDING MULTIBAGGERS

There is a term used in investing called *multibaggers*. It's a baseball metaphor which describes companies with spectacular growth and stock prices that advance over 100% for long term investors. These companies exist in Asia, and our investment strategy has been able to identify many of them for our investment firm. The following are some examples:

• • •

Li & Fung Limited was a link between the East and West in global supply chain management. Family-run by the Hong Kong Fung brothers, it sourced and assembled jackets and suits throughout China and Asia for a variety of brands located on US shelves. As one analyst described their unique value-added service operations:

> For this jacket sold by a trendy U.S. retailer, Li & Fung sources the microfiber fabric in Korea, the nylon taffeta lining

in Taiwan, the zippers in Japan from YKK, down filling from China, and arranges for the jacket to be stitched together in China… For a Robocop talking toy, Li & Fung does the mechanical drawings and sources plastic molds in Hong Kong, buys plastic resins in Japan, purchases customized chips in Taiwan and arranges assembly in China.[23]

We met William Fung our first year in Hong Kong and enjoyed his friendship very much. William, together with his brother, Victor, ran their family business, which originally manufactured Black Cat firecrackers in Guangdong Province and was started by their father. The company re-established in Hong Kong as an exporter of Hong Kong manufactured products when China turned communist. William and Victor listed shares of the company in 1973, developing trade in China after Deng Xiaoping became leader in 1979. The brothers took the company private in 1989, then relisted in 1992 after growing the export business.

William graduated from Harvard with honors and always seemed in good cheer. That was probably because he had things to cheer about. He and Victor were doubling the sales and earnings of the company every three years during the 1990s—one of Asia's most successful international companies.

William, who even taught at Harvard after graduating, was always very dismissive of all his successes. When I mentioned his honor grades at Harvard, William, in his amiable, humble manner replied, "Brook, that doesn't really matter that much. You see, A-grade students are bright and know a lot about one thing. They are hired by

---

23 "Did you know you were buying Li & Fung?" *Forbes*, September 6, 1999, https://www.forbes.com/forbes/1999/0906/6405118s1.html#430948383f15.

B-grade students, who are the company managers, whose bosses were the C-grade students that own the companies."

Li & Fung's stock sold at eight times projected earnings when we bought the shares in the early 1990s. Its market cap was just US$300 million.

In 1998, net profit reached HK$470 million (US$60 million) on revenues of HK$14.3 billion (US$1.8 billion). The market capitalization had grown to HK$10.4 billion (US$1.3 billion). Three years later, the market cap (in December 2001) had risen to HK$26 billion or US$3.4 billion on a doubling of operating profits.

Not until after several years of sustained earnings growth did large, institutional investors become interested and begin buying, taking the price-earnings multiple beyond thirty times by the mid-2000s.

Although Li & Fung was posting strong results, the company was vulnerable as roughly 80% of its clients were US based.

By the late '90s, the internet phase was rapidly growing in Silicon Valley. It wasn't prevalent in Asia when we urged William one day to think hard how his company might benefit from business over the internet. No other company had the breadth of knowledge of China and Asian factories operating in soft and hard good manufacturing than Li & Fung.

Though they did create a website for ordering custom clothing, it wasn't, for reasons we weren't privy to, an exercise they seriously pursued. The advent of business-to-consumer ordering over the internet was overtaken by China's Alibaba Group, as Li & Fung's major overseas retail clients, such as Walmart and The Limited, started suffering under the Black Star domination of Amazon.

From a split-adjusted cost, we began buying at HK$0.23 a share in late 1993. The company had been producing improved yearly results consecutively and as institutional interest in the company's shares developed, the stock valuation rose considerably. We decided to let go of our position and sell our last holding at over $10 per share when the market cap was HK$88 billion or US$11 billion.

We had a multibagger investing in Li & Fung shares.

A Galaxy Return

Another multibagger for us was Galaxy Entertainment—an example of a purchase and sale utilizing our proprietary intrinsic valuation screen we call the Banquet System. The Macau casino was (and still is) owned and operated by well-respected Hong Kong-listed property developer K Wah International, which is owned by the Lui family. We purchased shares in the first quarter of 2013 at HK$33 or fourteen times expected earnings per share. The shares were unduly depressed from growing fears of China's crackdown on corruption and many analysts questioned the Macao casino strip's future prospects. But gambling proceeds, in the former Portuguese colony, continued to grow unabated that year.

Galaxy's stock price rose and the company reported a 41% increase in profits in 2013. We exited our position in Galaxy after the stock rose quickly to our estimate of intrinsic value. We sold a year later amidst the return of analyst exuberance towards Macao in the first quarter of 2014 at ~$80 or thirty-four times trailing earnings.

Shenzhou

Shenzhou International Group Holdings Limited is an investment holding company principally engaged in the manufacture and export of knitwear products, including sports products, casual wear, and lingerie. They make jackets, vests, pants, trousers, tops, T-shirts, dresses and lingerie for fast growing brands such as Japan's Uniglo/Fast Retailing, Nike, Adidas, and FILA.

The shares of Shenzhou International were listed on the Stock Exchange of Hong Kong Limited in November 2005. We began buying at seven times trailing earnings in May 2010. For six years we held the shares, whereupon earnings had doubled, and then sold the last of the holding for a 370% gain. At seventeen times trailing earnings, the shares looked to be getting expensive to us.

That was a mistake.

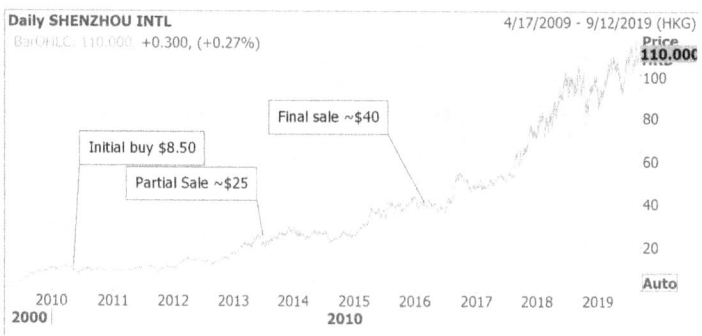

Today, the share price has more than doubled since our sale and sells at thirty-two times trailing earnings. It was a stark lesson to stay and hold onto quality companies until, at least, the institutions had become fully invested. Well managed companies in good businesses, priced reasonably, don't come easily.

Kingsoft

In the fourth quarter of 2018 we started buying a position in software design firm Kingsoft (code 3888hk), which sported a market cap of HK$18.1 billion, US$2.3 billion. Our reason for buying was that

Kingsoft is the leading PC/mobile games creator, the largest cloud service provider, and a top office software designer (WPS is a leading office software productivity suite for PCs). Because of a China policy implemented in the first half of 2018 delaying release of new video games, the earnings of Kingsoft have suffered, as well as its stock price. The shares traded one year ago at $30/share and have since plunged to a multi-year low of $13.

Kingsoft's share price, then at ~HK10/share, was selling below, or at a discount, from its fair value (on earnings) and was attractive on our screens. Our *Peter Lynch* valuation system uses the lowest five-year annual price-earnings multiple (of 19.5) times annual earnings (see the light line) as compared to the stock price (the dark line):

Kingsoft's cloud services and WPS businesses were growing strongly. We wagered that since China blamed the country's widespread myopia among children on playing video games, when China eventually allowed new game releases to gamer-hungry China fans (Kingsoft has 3.5 million active monthly gamers in the PRC, a country with close to six hundred million gamers in total), earnings would recover swiftly.

Since then, China has allowed new game releases and the share price has rebounded to the high teens as shown on the right side of the above chart.

China Everbright International

We began buying leading environmental development firm China Everbright International (code 257hk, market cap HK$47.5 billion, US$ 6.1 billion) after a rights issue raised HK$9.5 billion/US$1.2 billion in September 2018. The company constructs waste-to-energy power plants, methane-to-energy power plants, and sludge treatment projects. Its Environmental Water Projects division is involved in waste water treatment plants and its Greentech Projects segment includes industrial solid waste treatment and wind power projects. When we first purchased the stock, the company had ~HK$19 billion in cash after the equity financing and HK$14.3bn of un-utilized banking facilities (or ~$5.5/share), a sizeable war chest for future environmental projects. After the rights issue and share price decline, China Everbright International sold at 8.8 times 2019 expected earnings, down from its historic price-to-earnings ratio average of 22.4 times.

The shares remain cheap today using a depressed P/E ratio of 8.2x on the Peter Lynch system:

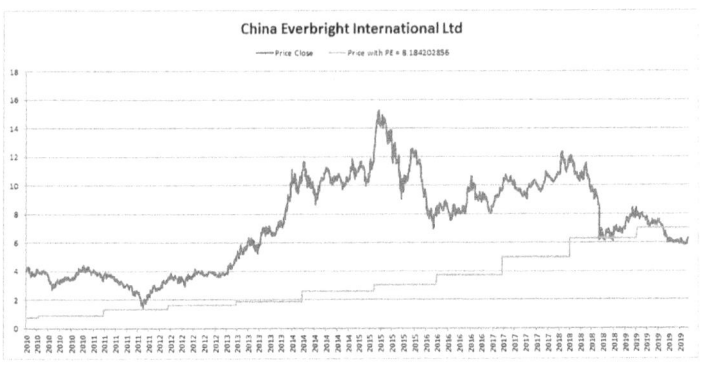

Beijing Enterprise

We mentioned above our long-time core holding was in leading water recycling firm, Beijing Enterprises Water (code 371hk, market cap HK$39.7 billion, US$5.1 billion). The shares were attractively priced on our Peter Lynch analysis in late 2018 as shown below (the light gray earnings per share line used BEWG's lowest average annual price-earnings multiple over the previous five years of 14.2 times):

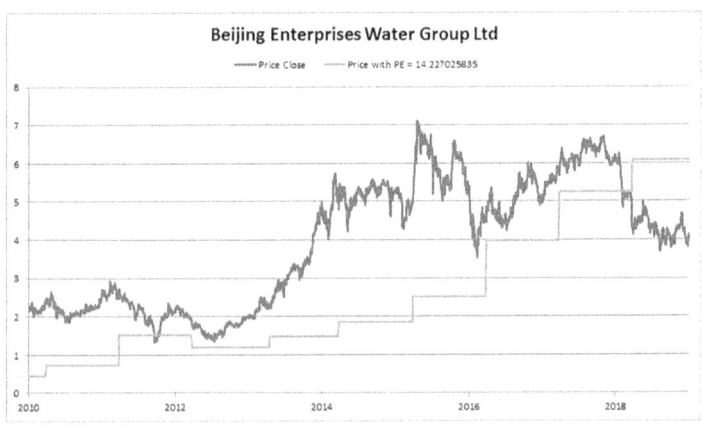

Net income had compounded 29% annually over the previous five years and management had stated it forecast 20+% continued growth for 2019. The shares sell today at 7.8 times trailing earnings (as of December 2019) and just 7.4 times estimated 2019 earnings.

If the P/E line in our Peter Lynch analysis is drawn with 2019's average P/E (8.5x), the lowest in the last ten years, the chart indicates the shares remain cheap today, even at a depressed historic multiple:

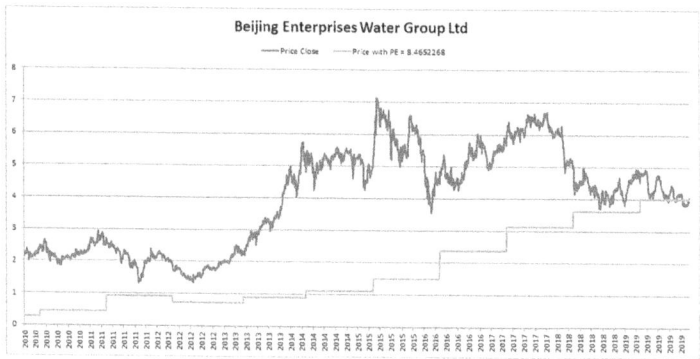

Buying growth stocks when the dark share price line (as seen in the charts above) falls below the light gray earnings line typically rewards patient investors handsomely.

CHAPTER 24

REFLECTIONS

We developed our investing systems in conjunction with the growth and transformation of China. Our focused and disciplined approach helps mitigate risks involved investing in Hong Kong, though doesn't totally eliminate them.

In our experience of dealing with institutions, here's a scenario to avoid: investment committee mentality.

Because most consultant, pension committees are run by hired people, they seek to save their important jobs. They have to answer to another committee of trustees, advisors, etc. and they can't be seen holding a losing position or relying on a trailing manager. Large accounts may be selling positions for reasons other than value and more about recent past performance. The resulting large flows of sell orders are one place where the best values can be found, especially in turbulent, volatile markets. Furthermore, there can be committees after committees reaching the same wrong conclusions at the same time. They're human, after all, and that's how markets behave.

Look at any 'fiduciary' pension manger's stock portfolio today and you will find the top five holdings are the popular FANG stocks. These fiduciaries have to perform, even on a quarter by quarter basis, otherwise the consultants (with piles of analysts' and strategists' recommendations on stocks/sectors) can critically execute dire pressure that might mean the end to a manager's selection. Many of these managers, therefore, are hugging an index or sector for fear of not performing every quarter.

For instance, one morning in the future, they may all wake up and find that the popular FANG stocks (Facebook, Apple, Netflix, Google) are down precipitously. They decide they should sell and invest in the 'less risky' sectors of the market. No matter that they sell out right at the bottom, they dare not be accountable for holding 'losing' positions. This explains one reason why markets can be inefficient.

This is what happened in the year 2000. Nobody knew March 2000 was the top of the market. Nearly everyone was fully invested in exorbitantly expensive new, internet-related companies. In fact, five years prior, every pull back in internet stocks was a buying opportunity. Then, after the top in March, many investors kept buying the subsequent pullbacks, losing all gains within a year.

Back to FANG stocks, which have been the main performing names in the bull market since 2009. Fully one-third of the 1,000-point gain in the S&P 500 Index, from the 2,000 level to the 3,000 level in 2019, was generated by only ten large cap stocks. The other two-thirds were accounted for by the remaining 490 constituents. A manager had to have been invested in just those few out-performing stocks to report 'out-performance.'

If you want to make above-average, risk-adjusted returns, go with smaller, independent money managers that can invest against the trends and withstand the immense, intense mantra of "I have to show continued returns otherwise I'm fired." To obtain above-average returns, it is wise to be leery of hired-hand, committee-run funds.

At our Hong Kong firm, we are fortunate to have clients that patiently allow our investment holdings the time to mature and become multibaggers. Our investment strategy is not complex, we simply seek quality businesses in growing industries that are run by competent mangers. They are smaller companies that can grow faster than large companies. It takes a bit more work to control the risk of holding 'junk' small companies that can decimate a manager's returns, but it's often richly rewarding.

...

As I've traveled through the hinterlands of mainland China, I have encountered many adventures as well as many dichotomies. I've been through small villages with barely any electricity and no telephone lines, and yet in the rice fields were tall cell towers newly erected. The juxtaposition of new and old has been stark. A farmer used to need three days to haul his harvest to the market to sell. Now, he gets price quotes on his crop from a cell phone before even leaving his fields.

I've witnessed abject poverty in the countryside, but the conditions were not like third-world slums. Communities held order, some of which were centuries old. I remember seeing an elderly man in old shabby clothes squatting on the worn-down, dusty curbside, cleaning into the gutter the last of his rice bowl. Maybe his conditions had always been desperate but his younger kin have much brighter futures. He is unlikely to become the next quantum computer engineer, but there are three hundred million entrepreneurial millennials anxious to seek and be a part of China's progressing society. The race is now moving from the starting lines onto the track. As a latecomer to the rest of the world, China is unencumbered by legacy technologies and long-standing gridlocks holding back advancement. It's like an artist's clean canvas readying for a masterpiece. China's competitive advantages are quickly evolving in a rapidly changing global landscape.

We continue to believe there is more risk in not investing in China, even if it is an authoritarian regime. I have many good friends living in Hong Kong and China. My wife is of Hong Kong Chinese heritage. And though many civil liberties are not yet available, one needs to decide if that is against one's principles or whether the Middle Kingdom will evolve to higher freedoms in the future as better economic conditions dictate.

As I've tried to outline briefly in this book, China's future looks bright.

Best to go East, young man.

BIBLIOGRAPHY

Asness, Clifford, Andrea Frazzini, Ronen Israel, Tobias J. Moskowitz, and Lasse H. Pedersen. "Size matters, if you control your junk." *Journal of Financial Economics* 129, no. 3 (2018): 479-509.

Carnegie, Andrew. Autobiography of Andrew Carnegie. Boston; New York: Houghton Mifflin Company, 1920.

Cheung, Eric. "Greater Bay Area: 10 facts to put it in perspective." South China Morning Post. April 1, 2019. Economy. https://www.scmp.com/native/economy/china-economy/topics/great-powerhouse/article/3002844/greater-bay-area-10-facts-put.

Dalio, Ray. "The Changing World Order." *The Changing World Order* (blog). LinkedIn. March 25, 2020. https://www.linkedin.com/pulse/changing-world-order-ray-dalio-1f/.

Déséglise, Christian. "Sell-off shunts some emerging markets into bargain territory." Financial Times. Dec 2, 2018. Opinion. https://www.ft.com/content/bba3fc26-dc39-11e8-b173-ebe f6ab1374a.

"Did you know you were buying Li & Fung?" *Forbes*. September 6, 1999. https://www.forbes.com/forbes/1999/0906/6405118s1.html#430948383f15.

Li, Keqiang. Report on the Work of the Government (2015). March 5, 2015. http://english.www.gov.cn/archive/publications/2015/03/05/content_281475066179954.htm.

Lynch, Peter, and John Rothchild. One Up on Wall Street: How to Use What You Already Know to Make Money in the Market. 2nd ed. New York: Simon & Schuster, 2000.

McConnell, Brook. "The Case for Hong Kong: It is Different This Time. Asset allocations to the region will rise and Hong Kong share prices are set to re-rate." April 14, 2014, http://www.south-ocean.com/monthly_updates.php.

———. April 2015 Client Letter, http://www.south-ocean.com/monthly_updates.php.

Micklethwait, John, and Adrian Wooldridge. The Fourth Revolution: The Global Race to Reinvent the State. New York: Penguin Books, 2015.

Negroponte, Nicholas. Being Digital. New York: Vintage Books, 1996.

Robbins, Tony. Money: Master the Game: 7 Simple Steps to Financial Freedom. New York: Simon & Schuster, 2016.

Sharma, Ruchir. "When the Bubble Bursts, Consider the Anti-Bubble." New York Times. December 29, 2018. Opinion. https://www.nytimes.com/2018/12/29/opinion/tech-bubble-bursting-stock-market.html?auth=linked-google.

Tully, Shawn. "Why Emerging Markets are a Screaming Buy." Fortune. November 20, 2018. https://fortune.com/longform/best-investments-2019-emerging-markets/

Welch, Jack. "Jack of His Trade." By Ken Aulleta. New Yorker, (November 5, 2001), https://www.newyorker.com/magazine/2001/11/05/jack-of-his-trade.

Welch, Jack, and Suzy Welch. *Winning*. New York, NY: HarperCollins, 2005.

World Population Review. "GDP Ranked by Country 2020." http://worldpopulationreview.com/countries/countries-by-gdp/.

"Xi Focus: Xi leads green development as world's largest horticultural expo opens." XinhuaNet. April 29, 2019. http://www.xinhuanet.com/english/2019-04/29/c_138019499.htm.

Xi, Jinping. "We will continue to advance along path of socialism, says Xi Jinping." Business Standard. May 4, 2019. Excerpts from speech. https://www.business-standard.com/article/international/we-will-continue-to-advance-along-path-of-socialism-says-xi-jinping-119050400676_1.html

Yu, Xie. "China's private firms shy away from bank borrowing, delaying investment." South China Morning Post. December 20, 2018. Economy. https://www.scmp.com/economy/china-economy/article/2178954/chinas-private-firms-shy-away-bank-borrowing-delaying.

Ze Yu, Shirley. "Donald Trump's WTO move is a feeble answer to the China challenge." South China Morning Post. August 8, 2019. Opinion. https://www.scmp.com/comment/opinion/article/3021667/trumps-wto-move-feeble-answer-china-challenge.

Zhengfei, Ren. "Huawei Founder Ren Zhengfei's Interview with Chinese Media." Interview by CCTV. https://www.huawei.com/au/press-events/news/au/2019/huawei-founder-ren-zhengfei-interview-with-chinese-media.

ABOUT THE AUTHOR

Mr. Richard E. McConnell, Jr.
President of South Ocean Management Ltd.

Brook McConnell (born 1952) co-founded SEC/SFC-registered investment management firm, South Ocean Management Ltd., in Hong Kong, where he relocated from the United States in 1992. He has been responsible for all operations in Hong Kong, overseeing client and custodial accounting, trading, analysis and management of portfolios. Before co-founding the company, he worked as an institutional securities broker with Melhado, Flynn & Associates in New York City for five years and, prior, as Vice President with PaineWebber, Inc. in Washington, D.C. for eight years. He is a 1974 graduate of the University of Denver.

Brook first co-wrote and published a book on investing in Hong Kong called, *The Investment Opportunity of a Lifetime, Hong Kong, 1997 and Beyond*. The book is based on the firm's philosophy of investing in the economic emergence and growth of China through the listed companies of Hong Kong entrepreneurs. He has written numerous articles for the local Hong Kong newspapers and appeared on Bloomberg/CNBC Financial TV programs numerous times in Hong Kong.

He lives in Hong Kong and Bozeman, Montana with his wife, Karolyn.

Email: brook@south-ocean.com
website: www.south-ocean.com

Info@south-ocean.com
Offc Tel: +852 2521-0332
South Ocean Management, Ltd.
GPO Box 1191
Central, Hong Kong

Photos taken at the
Sacajawea Hotel | Three Forks, Montana.
Photos by Randy Gallegos.

www.ingramcontent.com/pod-product-compliance
Lightning Source LLC
Chambersburg PA
CBHW050302010526
44108CB00040B/2109